The Monastery of
Saint Catherine
in Sinai

By the same author:

THE ANCIENT EGYPTIANS, *A Popular Introduction to Life in the Pyramid Age.*
The American University in Cairo Press, 1984.

COPTIC EGYPT, *History and Guide.*
The American University in Cairo Press, rev. ed., 1990.

SAKKARA AND MEMPHIS, *A Guide to the Necropolis and the Ancient Capital.*

UPPER EGYPT, *Historical Outline and Descriptive Guide to the Ancient Monuments.*

LUXOR, *A Guide to Ancient Thebes.*

The Monastery of
Saint Catherine
in Sinai

History and Guide

Jill Kamil

Maps and Photographs by Michael Stock

The American University in Cairo Press

Copyright © 1991 by
The American University in Cairo Press
113 Sharia Kasr el Aini
Cairo, Egypt

All rights reserved. No part of this publication may be reproduced, stored in a retrieval system or transmitted in any form or by any means, electronic, mechanical, photocopying, recording or otherwise, without the prior permission of the copyright owner.

Dar el Kutub No. 2761/91
ISBN 977 424 255 6

Printed in Egypt by the American University in Cairo Press

Contents

List of Illustrations   vii

Maps
    Map 1 Biblical Sinai   x
    Map 2 Historical Sinai   xi
    Map 3 Modern Sinai   xii
    Map 4 The Monastery of Saint Catherine
              and its Environs   xiii

Introduction   1

1 Geography and History of Sinai   5
    The Northern Coastal Zone   8
    Central Sinai   9
    Southern Sinai   11
    The Western Coast   13
    The Eastern Coast   13
    Changing Sinai   13

2 History of the Monastery   18
    Early Pilgrims   18
    Saint Catherine   21
    Sinai under Muslim Rule   25
    The Crusaders   28
    Napoleon's Restoration   32
    Sources of Income   35

3 Description of the Monastery   40
    Plan of the Monastery   43
        Church of the Transfiguration   44
        Chapel of the Burning Bush   49
        Mosque   50

Refectory	52
Bell Tower	52
Library	53
Icon Collection	55
Garden	60
Chapel of Saint Tryphon (Ossuary)	60
Guest Quarters	61
Visitors' Accommodation	61
Greek Orthodox Feasts	62
Codex Sinaiticus	63
The Environs	69
Mount Sinai	70
Mount Catherine	74

4 Biblical Sinai — 76
Traditional Route of the Exodus — 81
Northern Route of the Exodus — 84

5 Getting There — 88
To the Monastery from the West — 89
To the Monastery from the East — 90
Where to Stay — 91
Distances — 92

Selected Bibliography — 93

Index — 95

List of Illustrations

Facing page 1 Seventeenth-century icon of Saint Catherine

Between pages 34 and 35

1. The Monastery of Saint Catherine

2. The lower slopes of Mount Sinai behind the monastery

3. The monastery has all the features of a compact medieval town

4. The northern wall of the Church of the Transfiguration, with Moses' Well

5. The Church of the Transfiguration, with the Chapel of the Burning Bush

6. Sixth-century mosaic in the Church of the Transfiguration

Between pages 66 and 67
7. The peaks of southern Sinai

8. Mount Sinai

9. Pilgrims' Gate near the summit of Mount Sinai

10. The chapel on Mount Sinai at dawn

11. The view from the summit of Mount Sinai

12. The village of Saint Catherine

13. The Tourist Village of Saint Catherine

For Michael

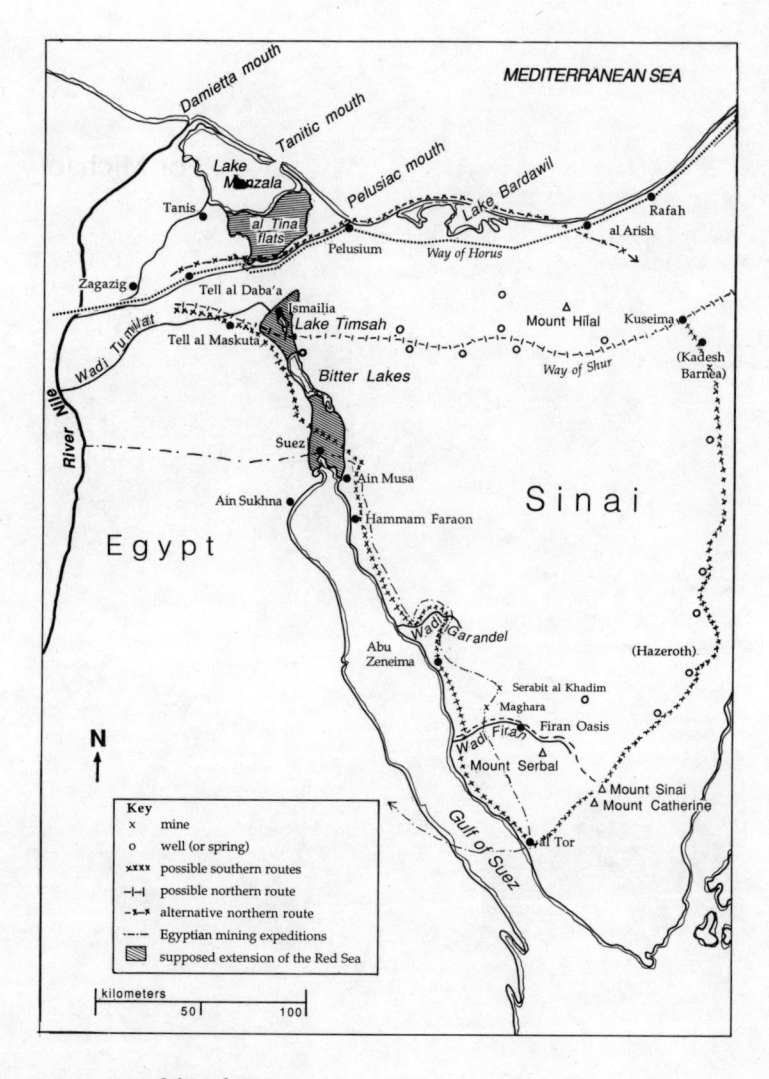

Map 1: Biblical Sinai

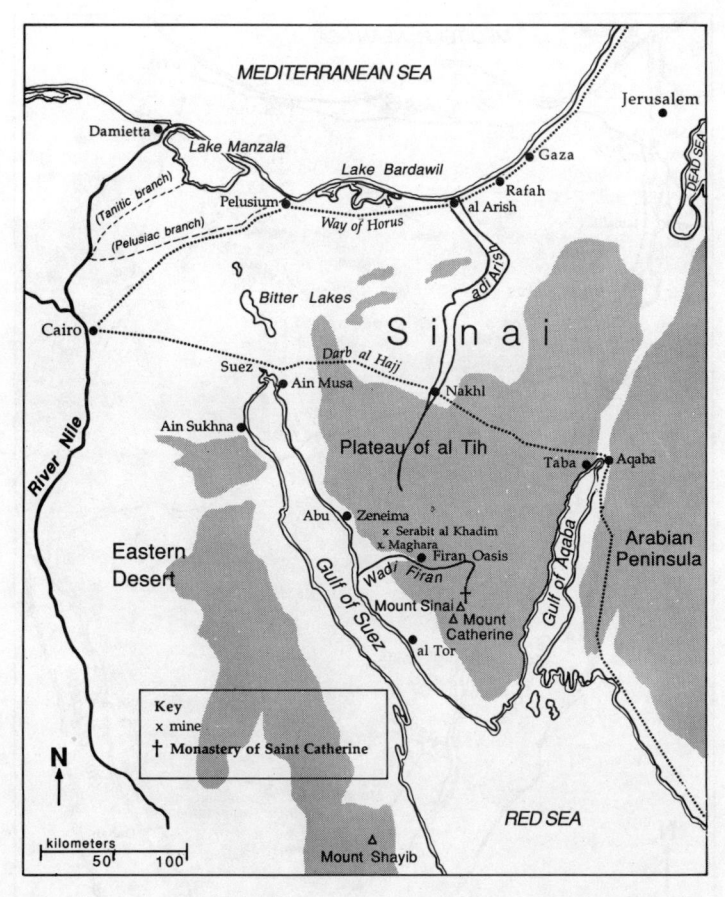

Map 2: Historical Sinai

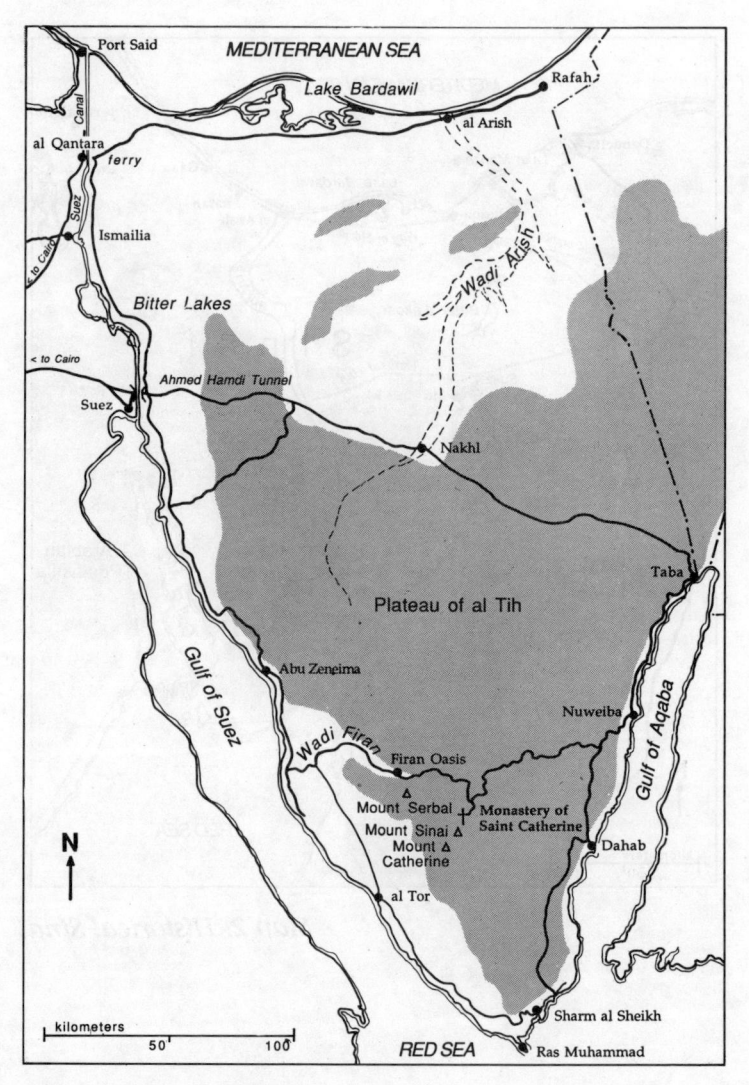

Map 3 : Modern Sinai

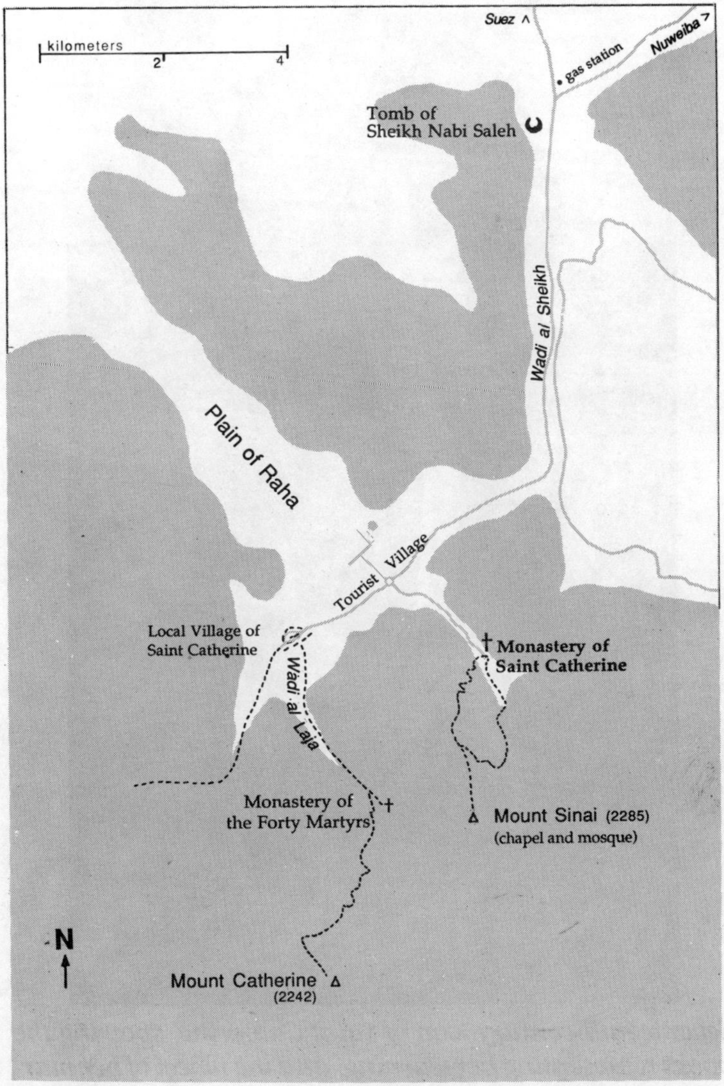

Suez
Nuweiba
kilometers
2
4
gas station
Tomb of
Sheikh Nabi Saleh
Wadi al Sheikh
Plain of Raha
Tourist Village
Local Village of
Saint Catherine
Monastery of
Saint Catherine
Wadi al Laja
Monastery of
the Forty Martyrs
Mount Sinai (2285)
(chapel and mosque)
N
Mount Catherine
(2242)

Seventeenth-century icon of Saint Catherine, showing the books representing her learning, and the wheel of her martyrdom, with the Monastery of Saint Catherine itself at her feet. Reproduced courtesy of the Monastery of Saint Catherine.

Introduction

The Monastery of Saint Catherine in southern Sinai, probably the oldest Christian monastery in continuous existence in the world, belongs to the Greek Orthodox Church. The monks practice the rule of Saint Basil the Great (c. 329-379), bishop of Caesarea and founder of many monastic institutions in western Asia. Saint Basil derived his knowledge of monasticism from monks and hermits in Syria and Egypt, among them Saint Pachomius (292-348), one of the organizers of the monastic movement in Upper Egypt at the beginning of the fourth century.

The Greek Orthodox Church, with its center in Constantinople (ancient Byzantium), once embraced a wide-

INTRODUCTION

spread community of people who spoke the Greek language throughout the eastern Mediterranean and western Asia, including Palestine and Syria, and an isolated outpost in Sinai which would become the Monastery of Saint Catherine. Although the lineal descent of the Greek Church is through the eastern Roman Empire, and not the Greek, it is a reminder of the time, before the dominance of Rome, when popes were Greek not Italian, and when Greek was the sacred language of Christendom.

The Greek Orthodox Church shares with Egypt's national church, the Coptic Orthodox Church, a common tradition that stems from the introduction of Christianity to Egypt by Saint Mark in the first century of our era, and the foundation of the famous Catechetical School of Alexandria about 190. Pantaenus, Clement and Origen were among the famed Christian scholars who taught there, and whose extensive writings influenced early Christian thought and faith. Only in the fourth and fifth centuries did doctrinal disputes split Christendom; after the Great Church Council of Chalcedon in 451, Egyptian Christians, or Copts, separated from the Greek Church and appointed their own pope and patriarch of Alexandria. The Melchite, or Greek Orthodox Church, nevertheless continued to function in Egypt, and thenceforward the two lines have continued: the Coptic Orthodox Church and the Greek Orthodox Church.

The Greek Orthodox Monastery of Saint Catherine in Sinai, however, stands separate from the orthodox churches of Egypt. Although it is doctrinally very much a part of the Greek Orthodox Church, it is separated geographically from the Greek Orthodox centers. It is the smallest independent church in the world. The abbot — who usually resides at the monastery and is elected by four archimandrites, by whom all decisions are made in a

INTRODUCTION

council — automatically becomes archbishop of Mount Sinai on his election. He is consecrated by the patriarch of Jerusalem, one of six ecumenical patriarchs in the Greek Orthodox Church along with the bishops of Alexandria, Constantinople, Antioch, Rome and Moscow.

The archbishop is in a unique position, in that he is abbot of the monastery and yet also holds the highest rank of the priesthood. He manages the affairs of the brotherhood and supervises the monks on a simple day-to-day basis, and he also represents the monastery at church councils as archbishop of Mount Sinai. His vestments as archbishop include the miter, a crown decorated with precious stones, the golden scepter adorned with carvings and precious stones, and the cross and golden medallion, while as abbot he holds a golden-handled scepter.

The monks of the Monastery of Saint Catherine, once of many different nationalities, are today mostly Greek, apart from a few Syrians and Armenians. Indeed, the monastic order of Saint Catherine is now open to monks of Greek origin only. Inheritors of both a tradition and an estate that goes back some sixteen hundred years, they have a great sense of loyalty to their heritage and institution, built as it is on sacred land associated with the Bible. They live together in a brotherhood of spiritual activity, starting their day at 4 a.m. with matin prayers and holy liturgy, and ending it with evening prayers between 3 and 5 p.m. They eat simply, once a day, during which one of their number reads aloud from texts of benefit to their spiritual growth. The work of the monastery is shared and divided amongst the monks according to skill and experience.

Living austere and remote lives, the instinct of the monks — some of whom are university graduates and masters of foreign languages — is to resist change. They

INTRODUCTION

have voiced grave concern about the increasing burden of more and more frequent visitors to their monastery, and particularly about current projects to promote even further the 'tourist potential' of their mountainous sanctuary.

One
Geography and History of Sinai

Sinai is the triangular peninsula that juts into the northern end of the Red Sea. It consists of an area of some 61,000 square kilometers, bounded on the north-east by a 200-kilometer stretch of Mediterranean coastline, and with the tip of the triangle lying 390 kilometers to the south.

Few places on earth have played so decisive a part in the history of mighty nations as this largely barren, sparsely populated peninsula. There would have been no ancient Egyptian empire in western Asia, no spread of Islam in north Africa, no Alexandria, no Arab conquest, had Sinai not provided a critical thoroughfare. It has known the marching feet of no fewer than fifty armies: pharaohs like Thutmose III and Ramses II crossed Sinai with their military forces, as did the Assyrian hordes, the Persian army of Cambyses, Alexander the Great with his mercenaries, Antiochus and the Roman legions, the Arab conquerors led by Amr ibn al As, Crusaders, the army of Napoleon, as well as Turkish, French and British forces in more recent times. On the soil of Sinai, both Egyptians and Israelis have known the agonies of confrontation and withdrawal.

Yet it is largely because of biblical tradition that Sinai is best known throughout the Christian and Muslim worlds. It is associated with the exodus, 'the wanderings' and the Mount of the Law of the Old Testament, as well as the New Testament description of the flight into Egypt and the return of the Holy Family to Palestine.

When the first Christian pilgrims, from the fourth century onwards, went in search of biblical sites, they followed a route out of Egypt that they believed Moses took. And they found, among the hermitages of southern Sinai, especially in the vicinity of Firan Oasis and Saint Catherine's Monastery, that a strong tradition had grown associating these places with the Bible. Only in the nineteenth century, when modern scholars and explorers studied the sites made sacred by tradition, did the suggestion arise of an 'alternative route' for the exodus. In the twentieth century, archaeological excavations in Sinai — and historical and archaeological analyses — have provided academic explanations that strongly favor a northerly route (see page 84). Convincing they may be, but the fact remains that the desolate majesty of southern Sinai is a far more dramatic setting for biblical history than the north, and one that religious sentiment upholds.

In order to reconstruct the early Christian setting, and place the Monastery of Saint Catherine in its geographical context, a brief description of Sinai will serve to emphasize its unique isolation, and to underline the current threats to its fragile ecology.

Egypt, Sinai and Arabia were, some twenty million years ago, part of the same land formation. There is strong geophysical evidence of this earlier fusion of the land: the mountains of Egypt's eastern desert, for example, and the craggy ranges of Sinai not only resemble each other, but are composed of lava in which mineral crystals of similar composition have been compacted. The highest peak to the west of the Red Sea, Mount Shayib, appears to have been part of the same lofty mountain range as Sinai's Mount Catherine; and the freshwater spring that once rose at Ain Sukhna, south of Suez on the western shore, shared the same source as Ain Musa on the eastern shore.

Then thermal currents in the earth's mantle created great tear-faults that lifted and spread the land. Northern Sinai sustained the upheaval and remained as the only landbridge between the two great continents of Africa and Asia. Southern Sinai, however, was torn from Egypt to the east, and Arabia to the west, leaving two gulfs: the Gulf of Suez and the Gulf of Aqaba respectively, the northern arms of the Red Sea. Within this isolated, mountainous and largely desolate region, early ascetics found the safety and spiritual solace they sought during the terrible Roman persecutions of the third and fourth centuries.

Although Sinai consists largely of a barren and irregular tableland to the north, and jagged mountains to the south, the peninsula is, in fact, so varied in its range of levels and contours, and so diversified in its composition that it defies simple definition. Scholars have identified no fewer than seven geological divisions, and the annual rainfall, which ranges from an average of 150 mm in the temperate north to only 60 mm in the south has produced, in places, fertile valleys and oases.

The Northern Coastal Zone
The northern coast of Sinai lies in the path of the great desert belt that stretches across the whole of north Africa from Morocco to the Syrian/Arabian desert. It is between ten and fifteen kilometers wide across northern Sinai. The now extinct Pelusiac branch of the Nile delta once flowed into Sinai's western Mediterranean coast, bringing fertility and urban development to north-western Sinai. East of ancient Pelusium are lagoons and large shallow saline lakes that lie below sea level, enclosed by offshore sandbars. The largest is Lake Bardawil. The eastern extremity of northern Sinai joins the Arabian desert beyond today's border town of Rafah.

The entire coastal strip of Sinai was once impacted earth made firm by marching feet. The 'Way of Horus', the military road leading from Egypt to Palestine in pharaonic times, was the main thoroughfare for the movement of people, the dissemination of ideas and the exchange of products. One can well imagine how the conquests in Asia, and the establishment of an Egyptian empire around 1470 B.C., heralded an era of intercultural relations; Egyptians traveled eastwards across Sinai to become residents of the empire, and foreigners came to Egypt as slaves, bondmaids, captives or students. A large community of Semitic tribes lived in the eastern part of the Nile delta in the triangle between Zagazig, Tell al Daba'a, and Ismailia. But often, when the chiefs of the conquered territories of western Asia brought tributes for the pharaoh, they journeyed across Sinai with their sons, whom they left in Egypt to be educated along with the sons of the pharaoh. There was close contact between Egypt and the people of the Levant in ancient times, and northern Sinai was the landbridge between them.

In Graeco-Roman times, northern Sinai remained as one of the main caravan routes for troops of mercenaries marching to and from Egypt, Syria and Palestine. Accompanying the armies were Phoenician merchants. World trade flourished under the Romans, and their unequaled route systems, including sections of prepared roads, linked North Africa and Roman Egypt with the whole of western Asia, and even to India and China. They built military posts of considerable size across Sinai, a day's march one from the other, or a distance of some twenty-two kilometers between them. The volume of trade across northern Sinai only diminished after sailors had mastered the monsoons of the Indian Ocean, and started transporting products from India and the Far East through the Red Sea to ports on the Egyptian coast.

Today, the narrow belt of northern Sinai mostly comprises silken sand dunes, which shifting winds often form into longitudinal shapes with sharp crests. The main cities on the northern coast are al Arish, Rafah and Gaza.

Central Sinai

A desiccated gravel and limestone plateau dominated by dome-like peaks lies immediately south of the northern coast, from which point the elevation slowly increases towards central Sinai and the massif known as al Tih. It is an arid plateau deeply incised with scores of broad *wadis* (valleys or river beds). Though none enjoys a perennial stream, many fill up for several days after a downpour of rain, especially Wadi Arish, the largest, over 200 kilometers long, which flows northwards and joins the Mediterranean at al Arish.

Despite its forbidding appearance, the plateau of al Tih has plentiful groundwater that appears in the form of springs, and at these points wells have been dug. Moreover, what appears at first to be a somewhat colorless expanse of desert is, in fact, fascinatingly diversified: flintstone covers the land so thickly in places that it resembles a glimmering sheet of crude oil; there are nodules of manganese in other areas, or even shriveled-looking stones known as the *sawan al almaz* ('flint of diamonds') that lie as though carelessly strewn about and, when split, reveal clusters of quartz.

When the active, strong, and vigorous desert community of Arabia carried the message of Islam to Egypt and North Africa, the *Darb al Hajj*, the route of the annual pilgrimage to the holy city of Mecca, lay across central Sinai. It is one of the tenets of Islam that all Muslims, once in their lifetimes, should make the pilgrimage, and caravans from Morocco, Spain and Algeria made their way towards Cairo, where they joined Egyptian pilgrims. The first leg of the journey lay between Cairo and Suez, where the pilgrims mounted camels provided by Sinai Bedouin, and set off across the plateau of al Tih. Nakhl lay midway across the peninsula, and from there the caravan continued to Aqaba before turning southwards along the Arabian peninsula.

Sinai was greatly developed in the Mamluk era, from the middle of the thirteenth century to the early sixteenth century, and the *Mahmal* ceremonies they introduced added focus to the pilgrimage to Mecca. The *Mahmal* was the an ornate litter sent with bearers to accompany the pilgrims and the Holy Shroud they carried. The shroud, a rich black and gold cloth made to drape over the Kaaba in Mecca, Abraham's house to God, was traditionally dispatched from Cairo with great pomp and ceremony, and touched for good luck by the people. The pilgrims and the bearers of the shroud were protected as they crossed the plateau of al Tih by a corps of armed pilgrim overseers.

The power of the Arab world depended to a large extent on their control of a vast trade area, and the Arabian peninsula lay between the Persian Gulf, Sinai and the Mediterranean. Road works were started, and Islamic monuments were built in northern and central Sinai. Consequently, the volume of overland trade was enormous. Only when the Portuguese rounded the Cape of Good Hope in 1498, did the key to world commerce pass from the Arabs to the Europeans, and Sinai's traditional role as highway come to an end. The flow of goods virtually ceased and the peninsula became almost totally cut off from the main commercial currents of the world.

Southern Sinai
Southern Sinai is a wild and tortured land of incredible beauty, which has tipped upwards — due to the eruptive folding and faulting of the land — to altitudes of between 750 and 2500 meters. From dry gorge and naked valley to sun-seared mountain peak, the rock strata run at all angles, attesting to the tremendous volcanic action that gave rise to the gaunt pinnacles. They creep one upon the other and are tinted with colors that represent ores and igneous rock:

azurite, a deep blue carbonate of copper; granite in hues of pink, yellow, and gray; limestones ranging from sienna and ocher to glistening white; and dark brown clay deposits, or marls, which form broad unstratified layers that give a striped appearance to many of the hills.

But southern Sinai is not entirely barren. Many of the *wadis* are covered fairly thickly with vegetation. Springs and natural wells are filled with infrequent but sometimes copious winter rains, which produce fruitful oases with palms and tamarisks. There are also flash floods, known as *sayl*, that result from sporadic rain which settles in dikes or natural basins; as the pressure builds up, the earth eventually gives way and the water rushes in torrents through gorges and ravines.

It was in these isolated mountains and fertile valleys that large numbers of ascetics from various parts of the Byzantine Empire, including Egypt and Syria, came to live, especially when Roman persecution was at its most severe. Southern Sinai was well beyond the sphere of Roman occupation, and the number of those who sought refuge there increased in the third and fourth centuries, when Firan Oasis — biblical Pharan, first recorded in the second century — became the seat of a bishopric as sizeable and splendid as any in Europe. The hermits were mostly from the Greek-speaking world, the first written documentation of such communities being found in the narratives of the monks Silvanus, Ammonius and Nilus who lived in Sinai between A.D. 350 and 420. Among the ascetics who retired to Sinai arose a tradition that the biblical sites of the burning bush and the Mount of the Law were located there. Pilgrims and travelers who later visited southern Sinai, perpetuated this tradition.

The Western Coast

The coast of Sinai that faces the Gulf of Suez is, to the north, a wide chalk and limestone area where swirling winds have fashioned the pale hills into weird and varied shapes. To the south, the land is rich in mineral resources including iron and manganese, petroleum and natural gas. The first successful development of the petroleum industry dates from 1908 when the Egyptian Oil Trust started drilling, but the presence of oil may have been known even as far back as 1500 B.C., when the ancient Egyptians used bitumen as an embalming material. This substance may have been obtained from natural oil seepages in Sinai. Certainly the ancient people exploited the rich turquoise and copper mines of Maghara and Serabit al Khadim, inland from the coast, having traveled across the Gulf of Suez from Safaga to Abu Zeneima.

The Eastern Coast

The eastern coastal plain along the Gulf of Aqaba is narrow. The bold highlands of central Sinai approach the sea, creating gorges of some considerable depth between broad belts of sand. From the tip of Sinai at Ras Muhammad and Sharm al Sheikh, to Taba in the north, there are reefs, islands and inlets. In places where the mountains jut into the sea, ideal conditions exist for the growth of coral reefs, which are unparalleled for the variety and richness of marine flora and fauna. In others, where the bedrock recedes from the sea, sandy coves and rocky outcrops abound.

Changing Sinai

Colonel Parker, a British governor appointed to Sinai in the second half of the last century, has provided the best

GEOGRAPHY AND HISTORY OF SINAI

record of Sinai before the wars and modern development began to change it. Author of *The Desert of the Exodus*, (popularized from *The Ordinance of the Peninsular of Sinai*, 1871), and regarded as one of the most outstanding figures in the recent history of Sinai, he carried out research into its history, flora, fauna, and Bedouin tribes, which showed a genuine depth of interest, and an unsurpassed understanding of the peninsula as it was before industrial development and tourism changed it forever.

Until the end of the nineteenth century the Bedouin population of Sinai, more affiliated ethnically to the Bedouin of Palestine and Arabia than those of Egypt, was concentrated in a limited number of places, mostly along the Mediterranean and the coastal belts of the two gulfs. The rest of the peninsula was largely uninhabited, although frequently traversed by tribes in search of grazing fields. Several factors changed this situation, not the least of which was the opening of the Suez Canal in 1869, which led to subsequent British influence in Egypt and, in protecting the Suez Canal during the 1914-1918 World War, brought armed combat to Sinai.

After the Great War, Sinai was never the same again. The Bedouin were jolted out of a way of life, perfected over centuries, by the chaos of a war waged on their territory. Not only did it disrupt their nomadic way of life by the intrusion of men and machinery moving and fighting over their land, but it introduced them to people and systems that were quite new, and naturally interesting to them. Readjustment to the 'old way' was not possible. Many of the young men had experienced ways which were more attractive, exciting, and profitable to them than a return to tending camels and acting as guides to pilgrims or odd tourists.

Another consequence of the war, and one that was far more significant, was that it proved to the modern world what ancient Egyptians had learned from their own bitter experience: that the Sinai desert was not an impassable barrier to invading forces. Although the Second World War, 1939-1945, affected Sinai little, its after-effects were drastic. When the State of Israel was proclaimed in 1948, the peninsula was destined to become a war-torn zone of contention. And the subsequent Arab/Israeli wars of 1956, 1967 and 1973 severed Sinai from the Syrian/Arabian desert as effectively as the Suez Canal had physically separated it from Egypt a century earlier.

One of the reasons that the Sinai Bedouin, heirs of thousands of years of nomadism, had managed to resist the march of time, was that they dwelt in a land that was not coveted, and they themselves were little exposed to materialism. This was now all changed. The discovery of oil fields, the growth of oil towns, and the settlement of Palestinian refugees, led to an increase in the population of Sinai, and to a wider distribution of population than ever before. The traditional Bedouin income, from cattle trading, acting as guides and hiring out camels, had been lost, but a new era of education and materialism had begun. Toyota trucks are a more familiar sight in Sinai today than camels, and corrugated iron shanties are more numerous than spacious woolen tents.

Industrial development and tourism have come to Sinai, bringing with them irreparable harm to the environment. The already existing scars of war — bunkers, observation posts and military debris in the form of abandoned tanks, lorries and crashed aircraft — have recently been added to in the form of oil spills and the uncleared leftovers of tourist projects. Sinai, which represents a simplified, and therefore fragile, ecology, is one of the most seriously threatened areas of the world. The Red Sea, that deep, narrow trough of water lying between Africa and western Asia is not only one of the globe's busiest thoroughfares, but contains, between its two arms, an area of enormous mineral and ecological wealth, and tourist potential: archaeological, religious and recreational.

It is not without forethought that the Egyptian government has planned for the political security and development of this strategically important peninsula. But the price of progress is high. Already Sinai, once teeming with game, is almost devoid of the larger antelope, and the oryx and ostrich are extinct. Despite control around coral reefs, there continue to be flagrant violations of the law. And many thoughtless tourists desecrate holy land with plastic bags and tin cans.

In 1981, an independently established Wildlife Office was set up in the governorate of North Sinai, and another in South Sinai. These are now working in collaboration with the Egyptian Wildlife Service (E.W.S.) which carried out a survey of the mammals, birds and reptiles of Sinai. Certain sacred, historical and scenic areas were declared to be 'protected', and to be regarded as reserves. Indeed, on July 31, 1983, President Mubarak signed legislation regarding areas for conservation in Egypt, specifically mentioning Sinai's Lake Bardawil in northern Sinai, Mount Sinai and the Monastery of Saint Catherine in southern Sinai, and Ras Muhammad at the southernmost tip of the peninsula. But there is a world of difference between a declaration of intent and real action. It is, in fact, a mere prelude to the setting up of a committee to define the limits of the areas for protection accurately, and to justify *why* they should be protected, before methods of law enforcement can be tabled. How well Sinai will manage to withstand the demands of development and tourism in an age of technology while all this is going on, remains to be seen.

Two
History of the Monastery

Early Pilgrims

Nestled in the heart of the stark and barren mountains of southern Sinai, is the Monastery of Saint Catherine, famed for its seclusion, its long history and its unique collection of icons and manuscripts. It belongs to the Greek Orthodox Church which is one of the wide range of orthodox churches (including the Georgian, Melchite Syrian, and Slavic) that adhere to the Chalcedonian dogma of Two Natures of Christ. According to early Christian sources, specifically a ninth-century patriarch of Alexandria named Eutychios, the first chapel on the site was built by Helena, mother of the Emperor Constantine. In 327, fifteen years after Constantine's famous revelation — his vision of the cross on the sun — resulted in his conversion to Christianity, Constantine and Helena traveled to Sinai. Helena, claims Eutychios, was so impressed with the site of the burning bush where, according to the book of Exodus, Moses heard the angel of the Lord from a "flame of fire out of the midst of a bush", that she ordered, in 330, the construction of a small chapel on the site. She dedicated it to the Holy Virgin. She also had a fortified tower built as a refuge for the hermits. A century later, a Spanish noblewoman called Etheria made a pilgrimage to Mount Sinai, and kept the first contemporary record of such a voyage; in her travel diary, the *Peregrinatio*, she wrote that she was shown the site of the burning bush, and that, "it is alive to this day and throws out shoots".

The fame brought to Sinai by subsequent aristocratic pilgrims and travelers from various parts of the Byzantine Empire also brought increased imperial attention, including donations, to the Christian communities, and as a result they were subjected to raids from desert tribes. This wealth, as perceived by tribes from Egypt's eastern desert, caused them to raid the Christian community. Known as the Blemmys, these tribes landed at the coastal settlement of al Tor, murdered the monks and hermits in residence in a church there, and moved inland. The local Bedouin tribes, the docile, gentle Towara, or people from al Tor, claim that while the Blemmy raid was in progress, a young monk managed to push their boats away from the shore, thus stranding them in Sinai where they were subsequently attacked and killed, in their turn, by a tribe from Wadi Firan. Ammonius, a monk of Canopus who journeyed to Saint Catherine's Monastery about 380, witnessed the sacking by the aggressive Blemmy tribes from Egypt's eastern desert of the holy site around the Chapel of the Virgin. He described how the monks were slain, only those who took refuge in the tower being saved. He also described a Saracen raid by nomadic tribes from the Syrian/Arabian desert who conducted a caravan trade between India, Arabia and Egypt. Ammonius, together with a senior monk named Doulas, and others, sought refuge in the tower while the raiders slew all the hermits they could find. When he emerged he counted thirty-eight lying dead in their cells, and another died of his wounds four days later. Then came news that forty hermits, as well as women and children, had been slain near Raithou (al Tor).

Firan Oasis (biblical Pharan) was particularly prone to attack. Having been declared a bishopric at the Council of Chalcedon in 451, it was the episcopal and spiritual center of Sinai, and the richest Christian community, until nomadic attacks caused many to retreat farther inland and join the community on Mount Sinai. There, the situation was little better. Nilus described another attack in the fifth century. He was one of the emperor's highly placed officials in Constantinople who, having visited the holy mount, decided to become a hermit. He and others of his spiritual inclination lived in cells on Mount Sinai, and only descended on Saturdays to spend the evening and the following day praying at the 'Church of the Bush'. On one occasion an attack took place, and Nilus saw fellow-hermits killed by the marauders, while others were carried off as prisoners. He helped bury the dead.

Such raids, looting, and murder continued until the sixth century when, responding to an appeal for help by the monks, the Emperor Justinian — one of the greatest builders in Christian antiquity — gave orders in 530 for the governors of Egypt to send architects and builders to Sinai to construct a fortification. He also presented to the monastery two hundred Egyptians and two hundred Wallachians to serve the monks as servants and guards. The latter were from Bosnia and they came, some of them with their families, to protect also the original chapel built by Helena, and their descendants still serve the monastery today. Justinian then ordered the construction of a large new basilica, the Church of the Transfiguration. Foundation inscriptions in Greek of the names of Justinian, Theodora, and (unusually) of the architect Stephanos on three of the wooden beams of the nave of the church provide historians today with the means to date the construction to within ten years.

Later in the sixth century, the monastery gained international importance when Saint Gregory of Tours (c. 540-594), patriarch of Antioch from 570-594, served as a monk there, and later, when Saint Gregory I the Great (540-604), pope from 590 till his death, sent a letter to John (spiritual leader of the monastery at that time), offering to provide furniture for a resthouse for travelers. Many pilgrims described multitudes of monks at Mount Sinai, bearing crosses and singing psalms. Some, including Antonius, also mentioned that many of the monks who climbed the mountain to make pilgrimage to the chapel on its peak, cut their hair and beards as signs of devotion.

Saint Catherine
Saint Catherine was for centuries one of the most popular Christian saints, though she is less so nowadays. She is understood to have died a virgin martyr's death at the

beginning of the fourth century, but there is no record of her before the eighth century, and her historiocity is impossible to prove; her legend, however, exists in various versions. Catherine was the daughter of a wealthy, probably noble, or even royal, family in Alexandria. She was not only tall in stature, beautiful and gracious, but also well-versed in poetry, philosophy, mathematics and languages. She surpassed all others in rhetoric and logic. For her adherence to her faith she was severely tortured, and eventually put to death. According to one popular tradition, she witnessed with grief how the emperor promoted the worship of idols, and tried to convert him to Christianity.

Many Christians from all ranks of society had suffered martyrdom during the terrible religious persecutions, especially in the reigns of the Emperors Decius and Diocletian in the third and fourth centuries. Catherine was among the victims who lived in the reign of Maximanus at the beginning of the fourth century. Although unsuccessful in her attempt to convert the emperor from paganism, she nevertheless astonished him by her knowledge. He forthwith put her under guard while he sent out a search for fifty learned men, whom he charged to dissuade her from her belief. They were unsuccessful. Catherine's arguments were so brilliant that the sages were confounded, and it was she who managed to convert them.

The emperor then decided that Catherine should be put to death. On his orders, knife blades were attached to four wooden wheels, which were set to rotate in opposite directions, two to the right and two to the left. To these the virgin was strapped, and the emperor ordered that they begin to rotate. But far from cutting Catherine to shreds, and subjecting her to a terrible ordeal, the wheels spun on their own and her flesh was not even torn. At this, the emperor decreed that Catherine should be beheaded, and his orders were carried out on November 25, 305.

At the maiden's death it was not blood, but milk which reputedly flowed from her wound. The Church of Saint Catherine in Alexandria is said to be the place where she suffered martyrdom, and inside the chapel is a block of marble believed to have come from the column to which she was bound. Saint Catherine is generally portrayed in iconography with what has become known as the Catherine Wheel.

Several different traditions relate to Saint Catherine's association with Sinai. According to one popular version, five centuries passed after her martyrdom before a monk in Sinai had a vision in which her body became radiant with light after her death, and was lifted by angels to a peak near Mount Sinai (subsequently known as Mount Catherine), where it remained incorruptible. When monks ascended the mountain in the ninth century, they found the intact body of the saint. It exuded a sweet-smelling myrrh that was periodically collected in small bottles because it was believed to have holy and healing properties.

In the eleventh century, tradition has it that a monk called Simon went to collect the holy oil, and remained with the body of the saint for seven years, praying that she might give him a part of her hand. Finally, three fingerbones detached themselves from her hand, and he conveyed them to the Abbey of the Trinity in Rouen in France. There they continued to ooze a kind of oil that relieved pain.

HISTORY OF THE MONASTERY

The martyrdom of Saint Catherine and the news of her body being found on Mount Sinai spread throughout Europe at the time of the Crusades. Indeed, the unlikely story circulated that the Crusaders returned to the monastery the three fingers of the saint that had earlier been taken to France. In fact, it was the presence of such relics in France, and knowledge of their healing qualities, that resulted in legends multiplying.

In 1229 King Louis IX of France built a church in the name of Saint Catherine in Paris, and the martrydom of the saint became so widely known that the monks of Sinai decided to bear the sacred remains from the peak now known as Gebel Katrin (Saint Catherine's Mount), and inter them in the monastery, whose renown as the Monastery of Saint Catherine became widespread at this time. The change of the monastery's name, from Monastery of the Holy Virgin to Monastery of Saint Catherine, is thought to have occurred in the tenth century, at the latest the eleventh. The Church of the Transfiguration contains her relics to this day: the skull and her left hand. The rest of Saint Catherine's relics were distributed in western Europe by the monks who, in medieval times, thus obtained assistance for the support of their community.

Saint Catherine's Day is celebrated on the anniversary of her martyrdom, November 25, according to the Greek and Latin calendars. On that occasion, a great procession and celebration is held at the monastery, in which the archbishop of Sinai and the monks honor her memory. Two golden reliquaries, the first containing her hand sparkling with rings and bracelets, and the second containing her skull, are carried around the Church of the Transfiguration.

Pilgrims, each bearing a lighted taper, take part in the solemn service. Many of them bear gifts and make vows.

Sinai under Muslim Rule

After the Arab conquest of Egypt in 640, the Monastery of Saint Catherine was an isolated outpost of Christianity in an Islamic world. The clergy of the bishopric of Firan abandoned the oasis and joined Saint Catherine's Monastery, where the lives and property of the monks were secured. According to tradition, a delegation of monks had, in the year 625, gone to Muhammad himself asking his protection, and the Prophet granted a covenant to this effect. He allegedly visited the monastery and never forgot the hospitality of the monks. In any case, the charter which resulted, and is known as the Covenant of the Prophet, was certified by the Prophet's closest associates, who are mentioned by name. The document is particularly important in that it expresses Muslim policy after the Arab conquest, stating explicitly that there should be no coercion or change of status of the monks, nor pressure on Christians generally. Part of the covenant, an authenticated copy of which is in the monastery, was renewed by successive Muslim potentates in Egypt, and states:

"If a priest or a hermit retires to a mountain, a hermitage, a plain, a desert, a town, a village or a church, I shall be his protector against every enemy, I, personally, my troops and my subjects ... One should not take anything from them, except voluntary contributions, without forcing them to do so. It is not allowed to move a bishop from his diocese, nor a priest from his religion, nor a hermit from his cell. None of the objects of the church must be used in the construction of mosques, not even for the buildings of

HISTORY OF THE MONASTERY

Muslims. He who does not conform to this would be going against God's Law and that of his Prophet ..." (From Meinardus, *Christian Egypt Ancient and Modern*).

Protection ensured, small hermitages, chapels and churches multiplied all over southern Sinai in the seventh century. Monks and travelers even described a prosperous settlement in Firan which, although badly damaged in earlier raids, had been resettled by military serfs and their families, who received supplies and clothing from Egypt. Their sole function was to protect the Christian areas in Sinai, especially from continued Saracen raids.

In 726 the Emperor Leo III banned all images of worship among Christian communities, and in 730 declared that they should actually be destroyed. The controversy over what did, and what did not, constitute a graven image resulted not only in wanton smashing of countless icons in the period known as the iconoclasm, but even in Christians killing one another. The movement had had its beginnings as early as the beginning of the fourth century — texts mention that images of the Virgin Mary, Jesus, and the apostles were appearing in churches and, mistaking the second of the ten commandments, about the making of graven images, a bishop called Epiphanius from Salamis had ordered the tearing down of icons — and only ended in 837, after the Council of Nicea in 787, where it was declared that Jesus possessed Two Natures, divine and human, and that, since the icons depicted only the human nature, they could be permitted. The iconoclasm raged throughout the Christian world, from Constantinople to Ravenna in Italy, and including Jerusalem and Bethlehem in the Holy Land, for almost four centuries, but it hardly touched Sinai. Isolated as it was, it was able to preserve its heritage, which is the reason for its possession today of the richest collection of icons in the world.

In the middle of the ninth century, Mount Sinai became an independent bishopric, and Constantinus, the first bishop of Sinai, took part in the fourth great Church Council in Constantinople in 869. The Monastery of Saint Catherine underwent restoration, and the mosque within its walls may have been built at this time. It is a square tower capped by a dome and minaret. Although not described by Arab chroniclers until the fourteenth century, the pulpit dates from the beginning of the twelfth century, and many authorities maintain that the mosque is, in fact, a great deal older.

Many cubical domed tombs of Bedouin sheikhs around Mount Sinai attest to the esteem in which the sacred site was held by tribes in Sinai that converted to Islam. In fact, the Bedouin of southern Sinai have a local saint known as Nabi (prophet) Saleh. His white-domed shrine is not far from the Monastery of Saint Catherine. The actual identity of Saleh is not known, but he might have been the founder of the al Sawalha tribe who inhabit the area around al Tor, some of whom cultivate land in Wadi Firan. The Bedouin associate the legends of Nabi Saleh with the deeds of the Prophet Muhammad, and annually celebrate a *mulid* to his memory. During the celebration, they cover themselves with dust from the tomb for luck, and leave candles, flowers and pieces of cloth there. Then they sacrifice a sheep at the mosque on the summit of Mount Catherine.

Towards the end of the eleventh century, Sinai became an archbishopric of the Latin Kingdom of Jerusalem, its Greek archbishop being suffragan of the Latin church of

HISTORY OF THE MONASTERY

Petra. And peace and stability continued to reign, even during the Crusades.

The Crusaders

The Christian warriors of the Crusades recognized the importance of Egypt as a power base for Islam, and having succeeded in taking Jerusalem from Muslim rule in the twelfth century, set their sights on Lower Egypt. Their aim was to hinder communications across northern Sinai between Egypt and Syria. Sinai, however, was largely unaffected. The monks had the assurance of the Latin Kingdom of Jerusalem that no harm would come to them, and they continued to live peacefully within Muslim territory. Nevertheless, to avoid exciting suspicion, they did manage to dissuade King Baldwin I of Jerusalem from visiting southern Sinai in 1117. For the next three centuries Christian Crusaders seem to have come to the monastery only as visitors, and they also took it upon themselves, as a special Sinaite Order of the Crusaders, to bring pilgrims to the holy site, offering themselves as protectors. Courtly westerners like Henry II of Brunswick, Philip of Artois, Duke Albert of Austria, as well as monks from Verona and Florence visited Sinai, and the monastery increased its external holdings. The holy places inhabited by monks were deeply revered by the Christian world, and the humility and self-denial of the monks was lauded. Some travelers described thousands of monks living near Saint Catherine's, including Ethiopians, Copts, Armenians and Georgians. When the celebrated Simeon I, archbishop of Sinai, and known for his mastery of Syriac, Arabic, Greek, Coptic and Latin, made a journey to Crete and Europe in 1203 to collect alms for the monks, he was extremely successful. He reputedly bestowed relics of Saint Catherine upon charitable donors, and the Count of Champagne is said to have received the whole hand of the saint.

The status of the monastery, however, began to be disputed. The archbishop of Crete laid claim to Mount Sinai in the thirteenth century, but Pope Honorius III (1216-1227) issued a bull in which he confirmed Simeon as archbishop over Mount Sinai and the neighboring dioceses of Pharan and Raithou (Firan Oasis and al Tor). These possessions were later confirmed by Pope Innocent IV (1243-1254) in a letter dated December 16, 1250.

After the fall of Acre and the Crusader kingdom in the Holy Land in 1291, the monks remained integrated into the Latin patriarchate of Jerusalem. Throughout the monastery's history, however, they had remained in touch with the see of Constantinople, and because the monastery had taken no part in the conflict of 1054 between the Roman and Orthodox churches, it also continued to be protected by the Roman Catholic popes, who conferred on it privileges that were confirmed in papal bulls. Indeed, a group of Latin monks settled in the monastery and built their own chapel, which became known as Saint Catherine of the Franks.

The monastery was in a unique position. It was more closely linked with the sees of Palestine, Constantinople and Rome, than with the Greek Orthodox Church of Alexandria. And it was protected by the Muslim rulers of Egypt. But reports on conditions in Sinai during the next centuries are vague, and sometimes contradictory. For example, the German traveler, Ludolph von Suchem, visited the site in 1350, and indicated unstable conditions.

HISTORY OF THE MONASTERY

He mentioned that the monastery was fenced with iron doors and fortified in every way, adding that it housed some four hundred Greek, Georgian and Arab monks. He described their devout, strict and chaste lives, never eating meat, rarely drinking wine except on special occasions, and limiting their diet to vegetables, salads, beans, dates and fruit. But later the monastery was described as extremely poor. Pero Tafur paid a visit in 1435, and found only sixty monks in residence, and he wrote that they were "in a miserable state". In 1479, Tucher of Nuremberg found the monastery closed and uninhabited, but wrote that he and his party of pilgrims managed to put up tents in the grounds. Yet only five years later, when the famous Swiss-born Dominican friar, Felix Fabri, made the pilgrimage in 1484, he described the monastery in glowing and picturesque terms, and mentioned that situated near the guest house was the Latin chapel where the monks used their own service books. He also described the splendor of the main church, which housed the relics of the saint.

The monastery continued to hold a fascination for travelers in search of the biblical lands. Striking evidence of subsequent western visitors are the numerous coats-of-arms and names elaborately carved into the walls of various buildings, particularly in the refectory. They date from the fourteenth to the sixteenth centuries, and are French, German, Dutch and English. Those who left records of their visits included Bernhard von Breydenbach, a wealthy lay canon of Mainz in Germany, and friar Paul Walther, a Franciscan monk of Guglingen, who much admired the pious hermits who chose to live their lives in the shadow of Mount Sinai.

HISTORY OF THE MONASTERY

The Turkish invasion of Egypt in 1517 did not affect the status of the monastery. On the contrary, it continued to be a protected area and, in the two and a half centuries under Turkish rule, even acquired possessions in Crete, Romania and Slavic Moldavia. The monks were, moreover, granted permission to sell their traditional wares of soap, wine, olive oil, vegetables and coarsely woven fabrics. Yet despite the fact that Sultan Selim built many fortresses in Sinai, and garrisoned them with Moorish soldiers, who were charged with the protection of pilgrims and the safety of Christian communities, the monastery was again subjected to serious Bedouin raids. And, again, there were conflicting reports of the number of monks in residence in the writings of various pilgrims and travelers. In 1582, for example, William Lithgow claimed that he saw some two hundred Ethiopian monks there, and mentioned that they were guarded from Bedouin incursions by one hundred soldiers. He mentioned, too, that the only access to the monastery was by rope and pulley, and that no-one could gain access unless the monks were willing to haul them up. But in 1600, a Frenchman, Henri Castale, found only one monk in residence, and described him as starving, although he did mention hermits living elsewhere on the mountainside.

The monastery appears to have been closed in 1618, 1632, and between the years 1656 and 1660. But in 1666, a reported seventy monks were in residence and, in 1700, fifty. In view of these unstable conditions, it is interesting to learn that in the seventeenth century, the monastery managed to extend its cultural and educational services to Crete — where the school at Heraklion was established — and later to Turkey, Romania and Russia.

HISTORY OF THE MONASTERY

Records reveal that in 1721 the monks built a chapel over the alleged tomb of Saint Catherine on the mountain that bears her name, and that it was divided into two sections, the larger part for Greeks and the smaller for Latins. Such evidence of national segregation within the Christian community is interesting in face of the continued spirit of toleration between Christians and Muslims in Sinai; a commemorative tablet on one of the towers of the wall surrounding the monastery is inscribed with the following words in Arabic: "Nicola Wahba, Moise Soliman, Wahba Ibrahim, Girgis came from Jerusalem to visit this holy place in A.D. 1675 ".

There was a possible threat of instability in Sinai when, in 1769, the Mamluks revolted against Turkish rule, but the monks remained neutral, and in 1782, the monastery gained full autonomy. Henceforward, the archbishop, elected by four archimandrites and consecrated by the patriarch of Jerusalem, became the spiritual leader of the smallest independent church in the world.

Napoleon's Restoration
During Napoleon Bonaparte's brief stay in Egypt in 1798, the monks of Saint Catherine's Monastery obtained protection from the French. The *savants* of Napoleon's army included a number of mathematicians, archaeologists, artists and scientists who carried out widespread studies in Egypt and Sinai. Among the places described in Sinai were Ain Musa (Spring of Moses), the sulfuric baths at Wadi Garandel, the acacia, mint, palm and tamarisk trees in fertile valleys and oases like Wadi Firan, and the Monastery of Saint Catherine, where two officers found only six monks in residence. They reported that part of the

monastery's surrounding wall and some of the buildings had collapsed, probably from the serious earthquake at the beginning of the fourteenth century, 350 years previously. On Napoleon's instructions, masons were sent from Cairo to restore the damage. The Kléber Tower, named after his successor in Egypt, was Napoleon's major contribution to the monastery. After the French were expelled by the British, Sinai was restored to Turkish rule in 1802.

Napoleon's expeditionary force in Egypt, and the publication of the *Description de l'Egypte* (an encyclopedia of Egyptian art and architecture, flora, fauna and society), brought to Sinai an ever increasing number of western travelers, including novelists, explorers and artists. When John Lewis Burckhardt, the famous Swiss traveler and explorer, visited the monastery in 1816 and again in 1822 (both times disguised as a Bedouin), he was able to report thriving olive groves and large numbers of pilgrims including Armenians, Egyptians, Muslims and, above all, Russians. He also saw the arrival of a caravan of eight hundred Armenian pilgrims from Jerusalem and five hundred Copts from Cairo.

The journey to Saint Catherine's Monastery was long, tedious and sometimes risky. An idea of how difficult it was for these early travelers can be gauged by the description of French novelist Alexandre Dumas the elder, who made the journey in 1836; he described suffering from sunstroke, sun blisters and thirst, and having passed "skeletons of dead dromedaries, whose flesh had been eaten by jackals". Nevertheless, his *Impressions of Travel in Egypt and Arabia Petraea*, published in 1839, did not totally discourage travelers. To climb Mount Sinai was the goal of most, and many wrote about their arduous yet rewarding experiences. An American, Henry Field, accompanied by another theologian, set out in 1882 with a pith helmet, goggles, and a huge umbrella. They retraced the route of the exodus to Mount Sinai. M.J. Rendell wrote a book called *Sinai in Spring*, and Arthur Sutton's *My Camel Ride from Suez to Mount Sinai*, followed by Rev. D.A. Randall's recorded journey, "from the great valley of the west to the sacred places of the east", heralded a rash of travel books. With the aid of the newly formed P. & O. Cruises, Europeans were able to make journeys to remote places, and a visit to the famed Monastery of Saint Catherine became part of the Grand Tour of the Holy Land. The monastery was depicted as a remote paradise, and westerners were enchanted at the prospect of visiting a place untouched by the modern world.

In 1844, Konstantin von Tischendorf, who was to deprive the monastery of its most treasured possession, the Codex Sinaiticus (p. 63) went there for the first time. Like all other visitors, he was warmly welcomed by the cheerful and hospitable monks in black robes. As a result of his published work, he brought greater fame to the monastery than at any time since the Middle Ages, and more and more westerners sought out its literary treasures, or came to sketch or paint the holy sites. Among them was David Roberts, who produced his famous lithographs of the monastery and Mount Sinai. Yet many scholars, like von Tischendorf before them, found access to the library difficult. They felt that the monks were being overprotective of their books, which at times they made no use of. In fact, they were well aware of the priceless treasures in their possession, which was the reason for their caution.

1. *The Monastery of Saint Catherine is a large, fortified structure that is totally dwarfed by the massive peaks rising above it.*

2. *Looking west: the lower slopes of Mount Sinai start immediately behind the Monastery of Saint Catherine.*

3. The monastery has all the features of a compact medieval town. In the foreground is the Kléber Tower, and to the right, the modern visitors' entrance under the gable housing the medieval winch.

4. Looking east down the northern wall of the Church of the Transfiguration, with Moses' Well in the left foreground.

5. The eastern end of the Church of the Transfiguration, with the Chapel of the Burning Bush in the foreground.

6. Central section of the astonishing sixth-century mosaic in the apse vaulting of the Church of the Transfiguration. Reproduced courtesy of the Monastery of Saint Catherine.

In the nineteenth century, Muhammad Ali (1805-1848), the founder of modern Egypt, looked favorably on the monastery and, following a, by now, long-standing tradition of Muslim rulers, continued to protect it. He allowed the monks a percentage of customs dues levied in Cairo for the maintenance of their religious buildings, and the monks felt secure enough to open a new door in their fortress. Throughout medieval times, the original large gate in the north-western wall of the monastery had been blocked for reasons of defense. Both pilgrims and provisions had been hauled up by a primitive winch within the walls, to an entrance that was well above ground level. The new door, to the left of the old, gave access to the monastery through a low passage at ground level.

Sources of Income
During the second half of the nineteenth century, the monastery lost many of its foreign holdings, especially in Russia, Romania and Turkey. The main source of its income remained, however, the Greek churches of Crete, Cyprus, Rhodes and Corfu. When envoys from the monastery went to visit the Catholic states each year, valuable donations were received. The example had long been set. Charles VI of France had given the monastery a silver chalice, and Louis XI had presented the sum of 2,000 ducats in fulfillment of a vow. Louis XIV of France, Queen Isabella of Spain, and the Emperor Maximilian of Germany also presented priceless gifts. Indeed, the opulent appearance of the church is largely due to gifts like these, and to others from the czars of Russia, including Catherine the Great, in the seventeenth to nineteenth centuries. More recent donations and precious gifts were bestowed by

HISTORY OF THE MONASTERY

King Constantine of Greece (who gave a magnificent necklace studded with diamonds) and Bishop Macarius of Cyprus, both of whom were staunch supporters of the monastic order.

The only real dependency of the Monastery of Saint Catherine today is in the coastal town of al Tor, the site of the martyrdom of the forty monks who were slain by the Blemmys. The Church of Saint George, built there in 1878, serves the small Christian community of that town. In Wadi Firan, the monastery — which since 1891 has functioned as a convent — maintains a large garden with a monk as custodian. It is adorned with stone capitals and fragments of Byzantine columns which date from the fifth century, and attest to the fact that there was once a large basilica in the region. The garden yields vegetables and fruit including mandarins, lemons, olives, pomegranates, pears and dates. The monastery has branches in Cairo, Suez and Wadi Firan, as well as in Cyprus, Crete, Constantinople, Athens, Tripoli and Asmara. In some of these areas property is owned, which augments the monastery's income, and supplies the needs of the religious community.

In looking back on the long history of this ancient monastic site, it is worth noting that time and tradition have only served to strengthen the thought and faith of the pious monks. For over sixteen hundred years, they have lived their austere and devoted lives, their numbers increasing or decreasing from time to time. In the years following the 1952 Egyptian Revolution, the number dropped to seventeen, and during the uncertain years following the Israeli occupation of Sinai and the eventual reoccupation of the land by Egypt, to a mere dozen resident monks.

HISTORY OF THE MONASTERY

Numbers notwithstanding, traditions continue. A custom that has survived since early times, is the feeding of the Bedouin tribe, the Gebeliya ('of the mountain') every morning. These free rations of unleavened bread used to be lowered by the huge wheel-and-axle device from the small gable projecting from the north-eastern wall ten meters above ground level. It is thought that the tribe may be the descendants of the Wallachian slaves originally brought to Sinai by Justinian to protect the monastery. They have embraced Islam, and have intermarried with the local Bedouin tribes, to the extent that they are now considered as Bedouin, and yet they are still somewhat isolated from other Bedouin tribes of Sinai, and show loyalty only to the monks of the monastery. Many live in tents nearby, some even outside its very walls, and they enjoy special rights and duties in the monastery. Along with their traditional Muslim feasts, the Gebeliya celebrate the feast of the Prophet Moses on Mount Sinai, and honor the Prophet Aaron and the Christian saints George and Catherine.

But other aspects of the lives of the monks are not so enduring. They voice real concern about the fact that the sacred sites of Sinai are threatened by tourist development. Their fear is not unfounded. For century upon century the monks have received with hospitality a stream of pilgrims, often many hundreds of whom would arrive at one time. But because, even up to twelve years ago, the trip from Cairo would take up to two and a half days' traveling, the flow of visitors tended to be spasmodic. Today, with a modern highway and an adjacent airport, visitors arrive at the monastery in their thousands, in groups of thirty to fifty, several times each day, and on every day of the year (that the monastery is open). The monks naturally resent their loss of privacy. An effort has been made to control the movement of tourists, with a limit on visiting hours and access to carefully controlled areas within the monastery. But new tourist development projects include a proposed vast new complex envisioned by the Egyptian government and private companies, which, if it goes ahead, may include the construction of a cable car to give visitors a bird's-eye view of the holy places. The monks view this proposal with considerable alarm.

Back in the autumn of 1980, conservationists were outraged when a Belgian, Jean Verame, pushed through what he called his 'Sinai Peace Junction'. Claiming to be an artist, his 'human dimension' was to spray thirteen tons of black and blue paint on rocks, peaks, boulders and valley walls in the Wadi Bir Nafekh, about two and a half kilometers from Mount Sinai, and in 1983 the first legislation for the protection of the sacred site was enacted.

Meanwhile, technology and tourism move inexorably onward. An article in the edition of July 23, 1987 of *Al Shaab*, the Arabic daily newspaper, claimed that "acute differences" had flared up between the government and the monks of Saint Catherine's Monastery because of the former's plans to establish these projects within the sacred area in which the monastery is located. The article outlined that "negotiations between the two sides to avert any clash in future have failed".

Little wonder. To the monks, any development which encourages mass tourism will destroy their age-old seclusion and the sanctity of the area, while to the Egyptian government, Sinai represents a valuable opportunity to diversify tourism and channel visitors to areas other than

Giza and Upper Egypt. The monks see any plan to carry modern technology to the top of its sacred mountains, including Mount Sinai — where Moses himself heard the voice of God — as an aberration, while the government sees tourist development as vital to the country's economy. The volatile situation was best summarized in an article in *The Observer* of January 21, 1990, which commented as follows: "... the monastic order that successfully outmaneuvred generations of invaders by converting them into protectors has finally come up against the heavy-handed bureaucracy of the Egyptian state". One can only hope that the need to protect these most sacred sites of biblical tradition will be recognized before it is too late.

Three
Description of the Monastery

The Monastery of Saint Catherine is a large fortified structure that is totally dwarfed by the massive peaks rising above it. Yet, in approaching the huddle of picturesque buildings within the surrounding walls, or viewing it from one of the nearby hills, one never fails to be impressed It nestles into the barren foothills, while plants and trees in the fertile gardens outside its walls grow in abundance. In fact, just as the cypress trees in the garden tower above the olive, apricot and almond trees beside them, so too the craggy mountains rise above the monastery. Mount Catherine (Gebel Katrin), the highest at 2,642 meters, is not visible from the monastery itself, but the lower slopes of

DESCRIPTION OF THE MONASTERY

Mount Sinai (Gebel Musa), which rises to a lofty 2,285 meters, start immediately behind it.

The monastery is set slightly above the floor of the valley and the level of flash floods, and its surrounding walls are of local red granite. The enclosed area is a somewhat irregular quadrangle of some eighty-five by seventy meters. And because of the uneven ground on which it is constructed, the walls rise, in some places, to a height of thirty meters. There is a tower at each of the corners, which face north, east, south and west, others in the middle of the north-eastern, south-eastern and south-western sides, and a sentry walk within the thickness of the walls. Many of the stones are carved with Maltese crosses that date from the sixth century, when the fortified structure was originally built on the orders of the Emperor Justinian.

The main entrance is in the north-western wall. The large original gateway, to the right, was blocked during medieval times for purposes of defense, leaving no entrances at ground level. A projecting gable in the north-eastern wall was the only means of access, and a small gate beneath it led, from the inside of the monastery wall, to a chamber that contained a mechanism comprising a huge wheel and axle which was used to haul visitors as well as supplies up to the monastery. It is still used today for pulling up heavy loads.

The new visitors' entrance is in the north-eastern wall, to the right of the Kléber Tower, and directly under the gable containing the medieval winch. A doorway leads into a foyer which houses an office for visitors' enquiries to the left, and several display cabinets containing various objects, including bows, spindles, and woodworking tools.

DESCRIPTION OF THE MONASTERY

The interior of the monastery, with its numerous buildings of various shapes and sizes, including chapels and cells grouped around small courtyards connected by narrow alleys and stairways, has all the features of a compact medieval town. Because it has been added to bit by bit throughout its existence, there is a lack of homogeneity about its buildings, even a certain incongruity of form: there are pointed roofs and flat roofs, square capitals, and round arches, a maze of vaulted corridors, circuitous passages and galleries, all dominated by the belfry tower. Adjacent to that, is the minaret of the mosque.

Apart from the main church, the monastery has twenty chapels, dedicated to the Five Martyrs, the Holy Virgin, and to patron saints. These chapels are only used to celebrate the respective feast days of each: Saint Stephen, Saint Antony, Saint John the Baptist, Saint George, Saint John the Theologian, Saint Tryphon, and others. Some of the chapels were decorated by Father Pachomius, who was instrumental in helping sort out and preserve the icon collection before he died in 1958. Within the monastery there is a large building that houses the library, as well as storerooms, mills, a bakery, a distillery, wells and guest quarters. As some early structures fell to ruin, others were built on top of them. In places, the lower structures have assumed the appearance of subterranean chambers. Every available space in the confined area has been utilized, and as one passes through alleys adorned with trellised vines, the carvings and inscriptions of those who have made pilgrimage to the site can be seen everywhere. The monastery is a living museum of bygone centuries.

The water supply comes from a number of wells, but in particular from the largest source, known as *Bir Musa*

DESCRIPTION OF THE MONASTERY

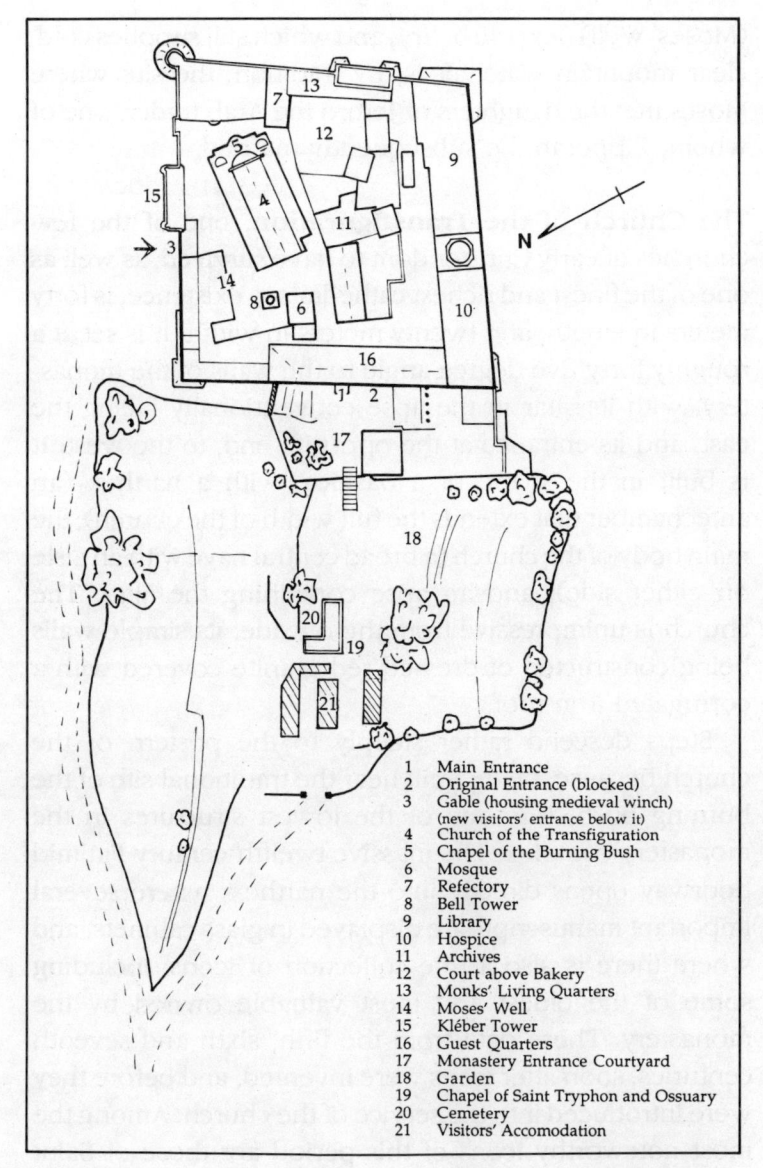

1 Main Entrance
2 Original Entrance (blocked)
3 Gable (housing medieval winch)
 (new visitors' entrance below it)
4 Church of the Transfiguration
5 Chapel of the Burning Bush
6 Mosque
7 Refectory
8 Bell Tower
9 Library
10 Hospice
11 Archives
12 Court above Bakery
13 Monks' Living Quarters
14 Moses' Well
15 Kléber Tower
16 Guest Quarters
17 Monastery Entrance Courtyard
18 Garden
19 Chapel of Saint Tryphon and Ossuary
20 Cemetery
21 Visitors' Accomodation

Plan of the Monastery

DESCRIPTION OF THE MONASTERY

(Moses' Well) near the belfry, and which still supplies cold, clear mountain water. It is, by tradition, the site where Moses met the daughters of Jethro the Arab trader, one of whom, Zipporah, he subsequently married.

The **Church of the Transfiguration**, one of the few churches of early Christendom to have survived, as well as one of the finest and richest cathedrals in existence, is forty meters in length, and twenty meters in width. It is set at a roughly forty-five degree angle to the walls of the monastery, with its altar in the apse conventionally facing the east, and its entrance at the opposite end, to the west. It is built in the shape of a basilica, with a narthex (an antechamber that extends the full width of the church), the main body of the church (a broad central nave with an aisle on either side), and an apse containing the altar. The church is unimpressive from the outside, its simple walls being constructed of dressed red granite covered with a corrugated iron roof.

Steps descend rather steeply to the postern of the church because, being built near the traditional site of the burning bush, it is one of the lowest structures in the monastery complex. The massive twelfth-century Fatimid doorway opens directly into the narthex, where several important manuscripts are displayed in glass cabinets, and where there is also a fine collection of icons, including some of the oldest and most valuable owned by the monastery. These date from the fifth, sixth and seventh centuries, soon after icons were invented, and before they were introduced into the service of the church. Among the most noteworthy icons of this period are those of Saint Peter, the Virgin and Child between saints Theodore and

George, Christ Pantocrater, three children in the fiery furnace, the Ascension of Christ, and the wings of a triptych of the saints Paul, Peter, Nicholas and John Chrysostom. One especially interesting work is the twelfth-century icon of the ladder of Saint John Klimakos (John of the Ladder), which was probably created in the monastery by an artist trained in Constantinople. John Klimakos is believed to have been a sixth-century abbot of Sinai who wrote a celebrated treatise on the virtues and temptations involved in climbing the ladder to heaven (see p. 54). The icon shows a ladder of thirty rungs, representing the thirty virtues; temptations cause many people to fall, and devils pull others from the ladder. But John Klimakos reaches heaven first, followed by another abbot of Sinai.

The impressive cypress wood doorway that leads into the body of the church is some four meters high with double folding valves. It is thought to be the original door to Justinian's church, and one of the few wooden doorways of the early Christian era to have survived. It has twenty-eight panels carved with such typically Christian motifs as the vine and tendrils, plants and animals of all kinds, including peacocks. It is inscribed with an extract of Psalm 118, verse 20: "This gate of the Lord, into which the righteous shall enter". One of the reasons that the doorway has survived in such good condition is that the decorative panels are set so deeply into the grooves of framing beams that it has prevented their removal. Some of them have the crests of Crusader knights carved on them.

The interior of the church is an impressive example of Greek ecclesiastical architecture and adornment, rich and opulent. The nave, whose roof is unusually high because the floor of the church, as already mentioned, is at the level

DESCRIPTION OF THE MONASTERY

of the burning bush, is flanked by six monolithic granite columns on both sides. Each of these is surmounted by a massive carved capital decorated with various kinds of foliage, especially acanthus leaves, though in some places, these have been replaced by crudely carved bells and knobs. No two capitals are exactly alike. The twelve columns represent the twelve months of the year, and to each is affixed an icon of the saint who is venerated each month. Those to the north represent the saints remembered during February, April, June, August, October and December, and those to the south represent those venerated in the remaining alternate months.

The capitals of the columns support arches and the upper walls of the clerestory, which is set with rectangular windows. Through these light filters to reveal that extending from the side aisles of the church are several chapels dedicated to saints, some of which contain relics: the skull of Saint John Chrysostom, the arm of Saint Basil, and the lower jawbone of Saint Gregory of Nyssa. The aisles end in chapels that are dedicated to Saint James on the north side and to the Forty Martyrs of Sinai to the south.

Between the columns there are elaborately carved thrones of the patriarchs and bishops, and the walls are covered with icons and paintings, some of great antiquity, and representing various episodes in the Old and New Testaments. Adjoining the third column on the north side is a pulpit, presented to the monastery in the eighteenth century, and decorated with beautiful miniatures. The episcopal throne near the fourth column on the south side dates from the nineteenth century, and is interesting in that it bears a representation of the monastery as it was at that time, held by the figures of Moses and Saint Catherine. It was painted by an Armenian artist.

The eighteenth-century wooden ceiling above the nave is painted green and adorned with gold-painted stars. It has two openings, in the shapes of the sun and the crescent moon, through which the rays of the sun and the moon are said to shine during Easter. The wooden trusses supporting the roof are original. The marble and porphyry floor was laid in the eighteenth century, the original having been destroyed during the sixteenth century. Suspended from the ceiling are no fewer than fifty vigil lamps and numerous chandeliers, thirty of which incorporate ostrich eggs. The huge bronze chandeliers were manufactured in the eighteenth century and presented as gifts to the monastery from wealthy benefactors.

In accordance with orthodox tradition, the nave is separated from the altar by, in this case, a gilded iconostasis. It was painted at the beginning of the seventeenth century by Jeremiah of Crete, and presented to the monastery by the patriarch Cosmos of Crete. Its four elaborately carved and gilded panels bear huge icons of Saint John the Baptist, the Holy Virgin, Christ, and Saint Catherine. The last shows the saint wearing imperial robes including a crown, alongside books that attest to her learning, and the wheel of her martyrdom. The iconostasis is crowned by a great crucifix that bears the figure of Jesus Christ painted in bright colors.

In front of the iconostasis are three pairs of tall early eighteenth-century candlesticks, and behind it is the sanctuary with the high altar. The marble altar table, inlaid with mother of pearl, is the work of a seventeenth-century Athenian artist. It is a large slab supported on six fine

DESCRIPTION OF THE MONASTERY

columns, the whole being encased in a framework that dates from the eighteenth century. On the altar are candlesticks and crucifixes.

The vault of the apse above the altar is adorned with the monastery's greatest treasure — an astonishing sixth-century mosaic, the figures standing out in exquisite shades of blue, green and red, against a background of dull gold glass. It is one of the earliest and most beautiful mosaics of the early Christian period, and is similar in style to that in the Church of Haga Sofia in Constantinople. The central theme is the Transfiguration of Christ, in which He reveals His divine nature to the apostles Peter, James and John in the presence of Moses and Elias. This theme is of special importance to eastern Christianity and is here depicted on a monumental scale. Moreover, it is in mint condition. Jesus Christ is at the center, flanked by Moses on his right and Elias on his left, with the three apostles Peter, James and John at his feet. Peter lies prostrate, but James and John kneel one on each side. Around this central group are thirty roundels portraying John the Baptist, the Virgin Mary, Old Testament prophets, and New Testament evangelists and apostles. Two angels hover above. Originally the mosaic would have been visible for the full length of the nave of the church, but today it is totally obstructed by chandeliers and the iconostasis which replaced the original screen.

Above the mosaic in the apse vaulting is a section of wall with two small arched windows placed centrally above the Transfiguration scene. These are flanked by a continuation of the mosaic in which the two famous Old Testament stories involving Moses are depicted. To the left of the windows he is shown bending before the burning

CHAPEL OF THE BURNING BUSH

bush to loosen his sandal, and to the right he is standing on Mount Sinai to receive the ten commandments from the hands of God. It is interesting to note that in this very early pictorial rendition, the commandments are written on a scroll, and not, as in biblical accounts, on tablets of stone.

To the right of the altar there is a marble sarcophagus or domed canopy, supported by four slender marble columns. It contains two richly inlaid silver caskets containing the relics of Saint Catherine. One holds her skull encircled by a golden crown studded with gems, and the other contains her left hand ornamented with golden rings set with precious stones. Beautifully engraved silver oil lamps burn night and day above the sarcophagus, which also contains other precious gifts presented by European nobility.

To the left of the altar is a votive sarcophagus, which also bears an image of Saint Catherine, wrought in pure gold and studded with precious stones. The two sarcophagi were gifts of the czars of Russia: Peter the Great in 1680 and Alexander II in 1860. Such containers were used to safeguard some of the valuable gifts made to the monastery by royalty and nobility of different periods, the emperors, kings, popes and bishops of Christendom who regarded the monastery and Mount Sinai with great veneration.

The **Chapel of the Burning Bush**, the most sacred part of the monastery, lies below and behind the altar of the church. It is approached by stairways leading downwards on both sides of the altar. The area was once an open space, perhaps a small courtyard at the end of the main apse, and accessible through the doors of the two adjoining chapels. When the bush in this courtyard was replaced by the chapel is not known, but a German visitor, Magister Theitmer, visited Sinai in 1216 and mentioned that the bush had been taken away and divided among Christians for relics, and that a chapel stood on the sacred spot. The plant was previously surrounded by a lattice fence, and is today protected by a stone wall, and although regarded as sacred, it is of a bramble species the like of which is not to be found in all Sinai. It neither blooms nor gives any fruit, although carefully tended by the monks.

The Chapel of the Burning Bush is a small chamber, three meters by five, containing a small altar upheld by four slender marble columns over a slab which marks the original site of the bush. This is where its roots are thought to be. The encaustic tiles on the walls of the chapel are from Damascus and of modern date. Unique icons and wonderful colored mosaics adorn the recesses.

It is said that sunlight penetrates through the tiny window above the altar of the burning bush but once a year, on March 23, when a solitary ray shines through a cleft in an unnamed mountain to the east, and falls directly upon the chapel floor (the cleft is marked by a wooden cross, called by the Arabs Gebel al Salib (or Mount of the Cross). In accordance with God's command to Moses, ("draw not hither, put off thy shoes from off thy feet for the place whereon thou standst is holy ground", Exodus 3:5) shoes must first be removed before entering the chapel. The holy liturgy is performed in the chapel every Saturday.

The **Mosque** near the belfry stands as evidence of the protection of the monastery by the sultans of Egypt, and also the monks' tolerant attitude towards Islam. It is a simple, rectangular building with two sturdy pillars upon which the arches of the roof rest. Although it is generally assumed that the structure was erected as a mosque, there is, in fact, archaeological evidence to show that it was originally a guesthouse that was converted into a mosque in the early eleventh century. This was a period of great danger to the monks. There were violent persecutions of Christian communities by the Fatimid caliph al Hakim (996-1021), often referred to as mad, and who was particularly destructive of churches between the years 1012 and 1015. According to one popular tradition, the monks built the mosque overnight, so that its minaret, rising above the surrounding walls of the monastery, would turn away any would-be Muslim marauders. Another version of the traditional story tells of al Hakim and his troops advancing on the monastery with the intention of demolishing it, when a deputation of monks and abbots went out to meet him. The sultan was so charmed by their eloquence that he promised not to cause them any harm, but to appease his troops' Muslim fervor, asked the monks to return to the monastery and erect a mosque within its walls. He also instructed them to inform the troops that in days gone by Muhammad himself had paid a visit to the monastery, and that the spot was therefore rendered sacred by the feet of their Prophet. Every hand was forthwith turned to the construction, and the mosque was erected speedily. Today it serves the religious needs of the Muslim servants in the monastery as well as Muslim visitors.

Inside the mosque is a pulpit with a kufic text that records that it was built in fulfillment of a wish of Abu Mansur Anushtakin in 1106. The minaret faces the church belfry. It is a detached construction nearly ten meters high. The local Gebeliya are entrusted with the keys to the mosque as a hereditary privilege.

The old **Refectory** is approached by a short flight of steps at the south-east corner of the main church of the monastery. It is a rectangular chamber seventeen meters long and five meters wide, with an arched roof in Gothic style, and it is lit by a single window in the western wall. The long wooden table, brought from Corfu in the eighteenth century, is beautifully carved with angels and flowers in rococo style. In the apse at the eastern end is a sixteenth-century mural depicting the visit of the Lord to the patriarch Abraham in the form of three angels symbolizing the Trinity. Both the outside and inside of the doorframe, as well as the inner and outer frames of the window, bear coats-of-arms of medieval pilgrims.

A small chapel attached to the refectory is liberally marked with graffiti by visitors from the fourteenth to sixteenth centuries. Other scratches and graffiti can be found on the pilasters and tables. The walls are adorned with icons and wall-paintings, including the famous Last Judgment (eastern wall), which dates from the sixteenth century.

The three-tiered **Bell Tower** is a nineteenth-century construction built by a Sinai monk named Gregorius. It houses nine bells of different sizes which were presented by the Russian church in 1871, and an ancient wooden bell which had been used earlier. These days the wooden bell is still heard daily, while the metal bells are used only on feast days or before Sunday liturgy. The summons to morning service is beaten on a wooden board called a *simandro*.

LIBRARY

*

A large new wing was constructed the south-western side of the monastery in 1951. It houses the library, the icon gallery, and a new refectory for the monks. The **Library** is a spacious and well-built fireproof concrete wing. It is over ten meters wide by fifteen meters long, and in the upper stories here, the precious codices and manuscripts are properly stored and shelved. It is off-limits to visitors. It represents one of the richest monastic collections in the world, second in importance only to the Vatican. It contains over six thousand volumes and manuscripts, three thousand of which are ancient, the bulk in Greek (over two thousand), and hundreds of others in twelve languages including Arabic (some seven hundred), Syriac, Armenian, Georgian, Coptic, Polish and Slavonic. The manuscripts — some of them older than the monastery itself, indicating that the monks either collected or were given these even before its foundation — include theological, liturgical, scientific and historical texts, as well as rare manuscripts in the form of rolls of varying lengths, sometimes reaching several meters. There are also charters or liberties issued by the caliphs and sultans of Islam in favor of the monks of Saint Catherine, as well as a large collection of books which were produced in the first decades after the invention of printing.

Towards the end of the nineteenth century a valuable codex was discovered in the monastery. What is known as Codex Syriacus is a translation of the Gospels into Syriac dating from the fifth century, and is the oldest translation of the Bible into any language. The text is a palimpsest, that is to say, a text partly erased so that the parchment on which it was written could be used again, as indeed, it was.

DESCRIPTION OF THE MONASTERY

In this case, the underlying fifth century text is now so faded as to be virtually invisible. Superimposed over the original translation is another text dating from the seventh or eighth century. Since the theft of Codex Sinaiticus (see p. 63) it is today the oldest literary possession of the monastery.

Among the manuscripts is a fascinating twelfth-century Greek treatise on the heavenly ladder of John Klimakos which, like the rungs of the ladder depicted in the icon already described (p. 45), is divided into thirty chapters corresponding to the steps of the ladder, each illustrated with monks in pursuit of virtues — not to mention the temptations to which they were subjected — and each providing details of how they should pray, venerate icons, and generally conduct themselves. The treatise thus provides a remarkable insight into the thoughts and lives of the holy community on Mount Sinai at that time.

Other treasures include a book of the Gospels dating back to the time of Theodosius III (776), written on both sides of sheets of white parchment, each sheet having two columns in golden rounded capital (uncial) characters, and the psalms of David written in minute calligraphy. All the books and manuscripts are arranged on shelves behind a locked grille, and are carefully guarded. The most important texts and exquisite miniatures and illuminations were microfilmed in 1950 by an international mission of experts. The rest of the material has been carefully cataloged and is available to scholars. The first volume of the series was published in Wiesbaden in 1970, and a handlist of Arabic manuscripts has been published in Baltimore.

The monastery also possesses a large collection of ancient and modern vestments embroidered in gold and

ICON COLLECTION

silver thread, as well as miters, chalices and trays of the finest workmanship, gold and silver crosses of various sizes and shapes, and illuminated Bibles of incredible beauty, in gold and silver filigree containers set with precious stones. These used to be displayed in a room annexed to the library, but plans are now being made to put them in a special museum.

The **Icon Collection** is the monastery's great artistic treasure. It is at present located in the wing that contains the library, but plans are underway for its transfer to more spacious and easily accessible premises near the main church, where it will be on permanent display. It is the most important single collection of icons in the world, and includes over two thousand works, one hundred and fifty of which are unique pieces that date from the fifth to the seventh centuries. The collection represents some of the finest Byzantine work from before the separation of the Latin and Eastern churches, and also includes a large number of icons from the period of the iconoclasm (726-843), when the depiction of the saintly or divine form in art was considered heretical. Elsewhere in Christian centers, all representations of religious figures in icons, mosaics and wall paintings were removed or destroyed. Only in the remote Monastery of Saint Catherine did so large a number remain unharmed.

It is surprising that whereas the literary wealth of the monastery was recognized from the middle of the nineteenth century, its valuable icon collection has been largely unappreciated until now, except by a few specialists. Indeed, the recent study of the monastery by the Sinai Expedition of the Universities of Michigan and Princeton in the U.S.A., in conjunction with the University of Alexandria, and including a specific study of the icons by Kurt Weitzmann, is the first in-depth study of its artistic wealth. The publication of Weitzmann's first volume of *The Icons* has already shed considerable light on the diversity as well as uniqueness of the collection. Some of the works were painted in Sinai, others imported from the provinces of the Byzantine Empire, and many brought to the monastery from Constantinople itself.

The earliest examples are masterpieces of the fifth, sixth and seventh centuries, many of which were painted in encaustic paint, that is to say in either tempera or water-based paint, or alternatively painted in colored wax manipulated with a hot rod. The sixth-century pieces are without parallel. Among them are a fine painting of Saint Peter, who has the penetrating look of a spiritual leader rather than a simple fisherman, one of the Virgin with Child between the soldier saints Theodore and George, a Christ Pantocrator which was almost completely painted over in the thirteenth century, and an icon showing an angel beside the three Hebrews in the fiery furnace. The last is the earliest panel of a biblical subject to have survived to the present day. Two of the icons provide interesting examples of contrasting styles of this early period: one is of Saint Paul, executed in the detailed realism of artists in Alexandria; and the other is of the Virgin and Saints, with the figures portrayed in the simpler, more hieratic style of Syria.

After the seventh century, when Muslim occupation cut Egypt and Sinai off from the centers of Greek and Byzantine culture, there was a weakening of the classical heritage. Then, when the monastery became more dependent on the patriarchate of Jerusalem in the ninth century, the contemporary icons begin to show the development of a cruder and more abstract style, with sometimes rather squat figures, and a tendency to crowded compositions. This is typical of the art styles in Syria and Palestine. Among this group of icons, the center panel of a wooden triptych (a group of three wooden panels) depicting the Ascension of Christ, is of particular beauty, as are a double icon of the Nativity and the Ascension, several scenes of the crucifixion, and an icon of Saint George.

The icons from the middle of the ninth century through to the beginning of the thirteenth (843-1204) once again show strong affinities with the sophisticated work carried out in Constantinople, and are elegant in execution. Indeed, by the eleventh century, large, monumental works of art were produced by Greek craftsmen from Constantinople, and a strong Byzantine influence is manifested in the tender expressions of spirituality on the faces of the holy people portrayed. Twelfth-century icons continue to show a marked Byzantine influence in the exquisite detail of clothing, gold backgrounds and tall figures. An important icon of this period is a diptych (two panels), in which all the saints of the holy year — more than a thousand of them — are shown on the two wooden tablets. Each minute figure is individually worked with painstaking attention to detail.

After the sack of Constantinople by the troops of the fourth Crusade in 1204, there was a halt in artistic development in the capital, and there is indication of a period in which no influence from the capital reached Saint Catherine's Monastery. Nevertheless, pilgrims from

DESCRIPTION OF THE MONASTERY

the west brought a wealth of gifts to Sinai, including icons painted by Greek and Latin artists. Among them is a large portrayal of the Prophet Elijah, and an icon of the Holy Fathers of Sinai.

After the fall of Constantinople in 1453, Crete became the center of what is now termed 'post-Byzantine' culture, and because the monks maintained close contact with the island, the influence of Cretan masters became dominant in the monastery. The monastery was host to an influx of refugee artists at this time, among them Latin monks whose influence is apparent in some of the work, especially that which combines the styles of western tradition with eastern rites. Icons painted once links with Constantinople were reestablished, again begin to show the refined later phase of Byzantine painting. Among the fifteenth-century icons many portray such themes as the Holy Virgin, the burning bush, and Moses on Mount Sinai.

Fresh and vivid sixteenth- and seventeenth-century icons by Cretan masters are extremely numerous in the monastery. They are characterized by more personal, individual figures, and brighter, indeed gayer, scenes and decorations. Among the most popular themes painted at this time were icons of the Virgin and Child and scenes from the life of Christ drawn from the Gospels. There is also a remarkable icon depicting the Virgin of the Burning Bush surrounded by Moses, Aaron, Elijah and Saint Catherine. The most renowned of these painters is El Greco, who received his early training on Crete, from artists associated with Saint Catherine's Monastery.

From the eighteenth century, icons began to be painted elsewhere — in Crete, Greece, the Balkans and in various parts of the Near East — and Sinai was no longer needed as a refuge, so lost its exclusivity in the history of icon paintings. Crete had become the great center for icon production, and its artistic output began to be distributed throughout the Orthodox world.

Because Sinai was open to Christianity at large, and monks from widespread Christian communities lived there at different periods, it is not surprising that some of their works should include views of the monastery itself, nor that the inscriptions on them should be in languages other than Greek; for example, Syriac, Arabic and Georgian. Indeed, some have bilingual inscriptions.

Two interesting observations were made by Weitzmann during his study of the icons. The first is that, although — or perhaps because — Sinai played host to artists from many schools, it seems not to have been conducive to a distinctive style of its own; most of the icons were either brought as gifts, or painted by artists trained in other places. There are only a few exceptions. And the second is that, although the icons at Saint Catherine's Monastery are many, and include masterpieces from almost every century, the collection does not represent a cross section of icon painting as a whole. It is, however, a representative collection of works made specially *for* the monastery, *in* the monastery by Syrian, Georgian, Latin, and later, Slavic monks who lived there, or *because of* the monastery — brought together under the very special historical circumstances of the monastery. With this in mind, it is not surprising that the most dominant themes should be the Virgin of the Burning Bush, Moses removing his sandals or receiving the tablets of the law, and Saint Catherine.

DESCRIPTION OF THE MONASTERY

The **Garden** lies outside the monastery walls to the northwest. It is fed by the spring that flows down the mountainside, but it owes its remarkable fertility to the untiring work of monks who brought soil from distant places, and constructed tanks and wells to provide irrigation and to trap rainwater. Formerly entered from the monastery by a dark passage immediately within the postern (now blocked) in the north-western wall, it is today accessible from the courtyard in front of the north-western entrance to the monastery.

The garden is surrounded by stately cypress trees and is laid out in terraces. Fruit trees of many varieties grow in profusion. They include oranges, both sweet and sour lemons, pears, apricots and plums, as well as vines and olive trees. When they bloom in March and April, the garden is a magnificent sight. The olives are either pickled, or pressed for oil, and some varieties of grape are dried into raisins, while others provide a rather rough but invigorating grape wine. There are also tomatoes and various vegetables which are carefully tended by the monks. Cattle and donkeys are kept within the walls of the garden, and the monks also breed turkeys and chickens.

In the center of the garden is the two-story **Chapel of Saint Tryphon**, the crypt of which serves as the **Ossuary**, or Charnel House. Because of the difficulty of digging graves in the rocky terrain, the bodies of deceased monks of the order are first buried in a small burial ground and later disinterred and placed in the ossuary. It is a somewhat grim place, with hundreds of skulls in one cage, and limbs and vertebrae in another. The bones of bishops and archbishops who either attained distinction or suffered martyrdom are placed in wooden boxes arranged neatly in niches. There is a fully dressed, seated skeleton of Saint Stephanos (Stephen) wearing a skullcap of violet velvet; he was a monk who lived alone near Elijah's cave, and who died in 580. The bones of the more humble brethren are piled from floor to ceiling.

To the side of the charnel house is a small area of the garden, less than four meters square, in which the bodies of the departed are buried for a year or more. The sexton then removes the bones to the great heap in the charnel house, where no one hermit's or monk's bones are distinguishable from those of his fellows.

The monastery **Guest Quarters** above the entrance, testify to the respect of the monks for the now-deposed Greek monarchy. Its walls are covered with photographs of the entire range of kings and consorts from 1863, even including Constantine I's German wife, who was also the sister of Kaiser Wilhelm II.

Visitors' Accommodation for casual visitors and tourists is provided in three modern buildings arranged around a courtyard on the north-western approach to the monastery through the garden, immediately before reaching the ossuary. Adequate accommodation is available for up to one hundred and fifty visitors at a time, in rooms sleeping up to six people. Male and female visitors are usually segregated. Within the complex are simple toilet, shower, and kitchen facilities, as well as a souvenir shop. Visitors who require accommodation should arrive at the monastery after 6 p.m. and ask for the duty attendant. Token payment of L.E.15 for lodging and food (one meal a day

DESCRIPTION OF THE MONASTERY

is prepared — if the monks are fasting, then so are the visitors) must be made, but visitors are advised to take with them any food supplies needed for the duration of their stay.

It should be noted that the monastery itself is open only between 9 a.m. and 12.30 p.m., and is always closed on Fridays, Sundays and **Greek Orthodox Feasts:**

January	1	Circumcision of Our Lord and Feast of Saint Basil
	6	Epiphany
	7	Feast of Saint John the Baptist
	30	Feast of the Three Hierarchs: Saint Basil the Great, Saint John Chrysostom, Saint Gregory the Theologian
February	2	Presentation of Our Lord
March	25	Annunciation
April	23	Feast of Saint George
		*Easter Monday
May	21	Feast of Saint Constantine and Saint Helena
		*Ascension
		*Whit Monday
June	24	Nativity of Saint John the Baptist
	29	Feast of Saint Peter and Saint Paul
	30	Synaxis of the Twelve Apostles
July	1	Feast of the Unmercenary Saints (Saint Cosmos and Saint Damian)
	20	Feast of Elijah the Prophet
August	6	The Transfiguration
	15	Dormition of the Holy Virgin Mary
	29	Beheading of Saint John the Baptist

62

September 8 Nativity of the Blessed Virgin Mary
          14 Exaltation of the Holy Cross
October   26 Feast of Saint Demetrius
November   1 Second Feast of the Unmercenary Saints
           8 Feast of Saint Michael and all Archangels
          21 Entry of the Holy Virgin Mary into the Temple
          25 Feast of Saint Catherine
          30 Feast of Saint Andrew
December   4 Feast of Saint Barbara
           5 Feast of Saint Sabas
           6 Feast of Saint Nicholas
          12 Feast of Saint Spyridon
          25 Nativity of Our Lord
          26 Synaxis of the Holy Virgin Mary
          27 Feast of Saint Stephen

* = *Movable feasts*

Codex Sinaiticus

Codex Sinaiticus — along with Codex Alexandrinus in the British Museum, Codex Vaticanus in Rome, and Codex Ephraem in Paris — is among the oldest and most precious codices of the Bible. Moreover, it shares with Codex Vaticanus the distinction of being one of the two earliest copies of the whole Greek Bible. That is to say, the New Testament in its original Greek, and the Old Testament in the Greek translation of the third century B.C. Until the middle of the nineteenth century, it was among the

63

DESCRIPTION OF THE MONASTERY

treasures of the Monastery of Saint Catherine in Sinai, and the monks were its custodians.

On February 24, 1859, Konstantin von Tischendorf, a German scholar from near Leipzig, gave the monks a handwritten note saying that he was taking the manuscript on loan in order to copy it. His actual words read:

"I the undersigned, Konstantin von Tischendorf ... testify by the present letter that the Holy Confraternity of Mount Sinai ... has handed over to me, as a loan, an ancient manuscript of both Testaments, being the property of the aforementioned monastery and consisting of 346 folia and a small fragment. These I wish to take with me to St. Petersburg in order that I may compare the original with the copy made by me when that is printed ... I promise to return it, undamaged and in a good state of preservation, to the Holy Confraternity of Mount Sinai at its first request." (James Bentley, *Secrets of Mount Sinai*, p. 98)

The monks counted on the return of the precious codex, but they never saw it again. Von Tischendorf took it to St. Petersberg where he presented it to the czar of Russia, Alexander II. Von Tischendorf later appealed to Archbishop Cyril, under whose rule the monastery had been deprived of its treasured possession, to ratify his gift to the czar, but no record exists showing that the monks ever agreed to this, or that an alleged sum of money they received was in settlement of the codex.

Von Tischendorf died in 1917, and the Russian Revolution in the same year resulted in financial problems for Russia which caused the precious Bible to be sold to the U.K. in 1933 for £100,000. The inscription on the case in the British Museum that holds the manuscript today reads: "'The MS was discovered in 1859 by the German Biblical

Scholar Constantine Tischendorf in the Greek Monastery of St. Katharine on Mount Sinai, and was subsequently presented by the monks to the Emperor of Russia". The monks deny that they had any hand in the transaction.

Much of the the secrecy and reserve that the holy fathers of Saint Catherine's Monastery exercise today is the result of their experience with von Tischendorf, who, though recognized as one of the greatest biblical scholars the world has ever known, nevertheless cheated the monks of their valuable manuscript. Little wonder that henceforth they have not only been reluctant to let anyone gain access to their library, but have been suspicious of scholars, especially westerners, who wished to inspect their archives, even if they held the highest credentials. Since von Tischendorf, those who wish to work in the library have first to obtain letters of recommendation to the librarian of the monastery from the archbishop of Sinai, and attempts have not always been successful.

Von Tischendorf's quest for new sources of the authentic Gospels had already taken him to many countries before he turned his attention to Sinai. He had a compulsive desire to search for the earliest version of the New Testament. He believed that the first text came from the hand of the apostles themselves, but had been copied again and again until the original passages were so seriously modified as to leave later generations uncertain of what had actually been written. He was convinced that an early version existed, and that when it was found it would prove to be the least corrupt of all manuscripts hitherto identified.

Von Tischendorf made his first journey to Saint Cather-

DESCRIPTION OF THE MONASTERY

ine's Monastery in 1844, when he saw some eighty parchments, and managed to take fifty-three with him to Leipzig, in January 1845. He published these a year later, under the title Codex Frederico-Augustanus, nowhere making mention of where he had obtained them. When he made his way to Sinai a second time, in 1852, the monks were less welcoming, and von Tischendorf came away empty-handed. Like many western scholars in the nineteenth century, he felt that they were being overprotective of their books, and that they never used them. In fact, the monks were well aware of the value of their possessions, which was the reason for their reserve.

Undaunted, and certain that the monastery housed unknown literary treasures in addition to those he had already seen, von Tischendorf sought and obtained funds from the czar of Russia, Alexander II, for another journey to Sinai, promising to present to him whatever he could bring back. His third visit to the monastery, in 1859, reaped its reward. Von Tischendorf was shown a large parcel that proved to contain well over three hundred parchments. He studied the Greek text by candlelight, and carefully began to copy it, quickly recognizing that it comprised not just the Old Testament but also the whole of the New. Neither the Codex Vaticanus nor the London Alexandrinus was so complete, and von Tischendorf was immensely excited, and convinced that he would gain lasting renown by revealing its contents to the Christian world.

He then embarked on what James Bentley describes in his *Secrets of Mount Sinai* as, "the remarkable piece of duplicity which was to occupy him for the next decade, which involved the careful suppression of facts and the systematic denigration of the monks on Mount Sinai". By

7. *The peaks of southern Sinai. Mount Catherine, to the left, tops them all.*

8. *Mount Sinai, or Gebel Musa. The higher peak of Mount Catherine can be seen in the background.*

9. *Pilgrims' Gate near the summit of Mount Sinai.*

10. *The chapel on Mount Sinai at dawn.*

11. *The view from the summit of Mount Sinai.*

12. The compact local village of Saint Catherine.

13. The Tourist Village of Saint Catherine, built of natural stone to blend aesthetically with the surrounding landscape.

falsely earning the confidence of the holy fathers in his endeavors, von Tischendorf managed to get the codex out of the hands of its owners, and he returned to St. Petersburg in triumph. On November 19, 1859, he wrote, "I presented to their Imperial Majesties .... my rich collection of .... manuscripts, in the middle of which the Sinaitic Bible shone like a crown". It apparently disturbed von Tischendorf not at all that the gift to Alexander II and the czarina had not been his to give in the first place. And the copy of the entire work, reproduced at the expense of the czar, and presented to the monastery, was a poor substitute for the original.

A ruthless man he might have been, but this did not alter the fact that von Tischendorf was also a brilliant scholar. When he started to translate the Codex Sinaiticus, he realized that he had been right. He had found the oldest uncorrupted text of the Holy Scripture. Philological evidence pointed to its being a very early production of the Christian era, and he was determined to make its significance known. He produced the first publication of the codex in an astoundingly short time, in 1862 bringing out three folio volumes of the text, as well as a separate commentary on the work. Moreover, he was able to identify no fewer than four different handwritings of the original text from which the codex was produced. These handwritings, he was sure, were those of four scribes who had written from dictation.

The great significance of the Codex Sinaiticus is that it is the only known copy of the Greek New Testament in its original uncial script. It is not known exactly where the codex was originally written. It was certainly not in the monastery where it was found, since it had not then been built. There is some indication, but no conclusive proof, that it was originally written in Caesarea on the Phoenician coast, possibly after Constantine the Great decided that Christianity could be one of the permitted religions in his empire. In an attempt to spread the Christian faith based on sacred scriptures, he ordered Eusebius of Caesarea, in the year 331, to arrange for the production by professional scribes of fifty manuscripts of the Bible on parchment. Eusebius ran a 'scriptorium' at Constantinople, and presumably responded to the request. It is thought that both the Codex Sinaiticus and Codex Vaticanus were among those produced on the emperor's orders.

The discovery of the Codex Sinaiticus revolutionized biblical analysis. Before its discovery, von Tischendorf and other scholars had believed the Gospel according to Matthew was earlier than Mark's, and that John and Matthew had been direct eye-witnesses to the events in the life of Jesus. Study of the codex led him to think otherwise. Through brilliant literary detective work, von Tischendorf studied the order of events in the ancient texts, compared biblical stories, and provided evidence — subsequently hotly disputed but today generally accepted — that the Gospel of Mark was written before those of Matthew and Luke. John's Gospel proved difficult to place precisely. Accepting that the Gospel according to Mark is the oldest, it is startling to learn that some of the most treasured biblical stories do not appear in it. They may, consequently, be later additions. Controversies and theological disputes have raged since von Tischendorf's day, and are bound to continue.

On May 26, 1975, a remarkable discovery was made by the monks of Saint Catherine's. A room in the great north-western wall was being cleared after a fire in the chapel of Saint George, and it proved to contain a hoard of manuscripts. Until the eighteenth century, a part of the library had been kept there, and when most of the codices and manuscripts — especially those in Greek — were later moved, some had been left behind. This collection, mostly Syrian and Slavic texts, was subsequently buried when the roof caved in. Interestingly, among the manuscripts that came to light were some dozen leaves that the monks recognized as being part of the Codex Sinaiticus. Today, the fifty-three leaves originally purloined by von Tischendorf are preserved in Leipzig, 346 leaves and a fragment are in the British Museum, and the dozen newly discovered leaves remain in the Monastery of Saint Catherine.

After the discovery, the monks contacted the Greek Ministry of Culture and Science, and in 1976 and 1977 experts from the National Library of Athens, and other conservationists, traveled to Sinai. At the International Byzantine Congress in Vienna in October 1981, the find was made public for the first time, and Archbishop Damianos announced that the discovery would be made available to scholars after the monastery had published its own catalog.

The full significance of the newly discovered collection is not yet known, but the texts are expected to shed more light on the early Christian era.

The Environs

The silence and stillness of the desert in southern Sinai is sometimes unbroken, even by the wind, for days on end. It was perhaps this characteristic, more than any other, which caused it to be a favorite dwelling place of hermits early in the Christian era. The coloring of the mountains is spectacular, their stratification, faults and veins vivid and dramatic, and this aspect has inspired artists and writers to explore the environs no less keenly than pilgrims. Even the laying down of modern highways across southern Sinai, streamlining tracks and erecting signposts, has detracted little from the beauty of the area.

Although rainfall is spasmodic, and greenery rarely seen except in oases, many varieties of fragrant desert herbs and shrubs are to be found. It is surprising that so thin a coating of vegetation should furnish sufficient pasturage for the camels, goats and sheep that form the Bedouin herds, but such is the case. The rugged hillsides are not wholly devoid of plant life, a fact which contributes, in no small degree, to the livelihood of the tribes who live in the region. Different varieties grow at different altitudes even on the most rough and unyielding surfaces. Most spectacular, however, is the seemingly instantaneous transformation caused by rain. No-one who has traveled in Sinai can forget the fragrance of unseen incense, or the sight of the normally barren wasteland, with its sparse clothing of thorny bushes and shrubs, turning overnight into a carpet of verdure and flowers after unexpected rainfall.

The exhilarating effect of the fresh morning air of the region at any time, is such that few visitors can resist the temptation to trek up at least one of the two famed mountains of the region.

Mount Sinai (Gebel Musa)
Made sacred by tradition, Mount Sinai is honored by the three great monotheistic religions of the world: Judaism,

THE ENVIRONS

Christianity and Islam. It is an almost isolated peak, 2,244 meters high, at the southern extremity of a lofty plateau. The lower slopes of the mountain rise behind the Monastery of Saint Catherine, bounded to the west by Wadi al Laja (Valley of Refuge), to the east by Wadi al Deir (Valley of the Monastery), and with the Plain of Raha spreading out at its base.

According to Christian tradition, Mount Sinai is Mount Horeb of the Bible, where Moses received the tablets of the law inscribed with the ten commandments. Although several paths lead to the summit, the one most frequently used is known as *sikket Sayidna Musa*, or 'path of our Lord Moses'. It commences immediately behind the monastery, where a steep ravine leads in a southerly direction towards the foot of the mountain. Most visitors make the ascent before dawn, in order to enjoy the sunrise from the peak of the sacred mountain. Consequently, they miss many attractive landmarks on their way up. Those with more time, however, can also make the pilgrimage in the daytime, and enjoy the gentle, graded path that leads upwards to the first landmark, a well in a granite rock edged with green moss and supplying crystal clear water. It is known as *mayet Musa*, or 'water of Moses', and the monks regard it as the spring created for the cobbler Sargarius, a saint who lived there.

A further ascent leads to a narrow platform where there is a small stone chapel dedicated to the Virgin Mary. It was built in commemoration of a miraculous event: a caravan of food for the monastery was once delayed, and there was little left in the storerooms, so the monks decided to walk up the holy mountain to offer prayers. When they reached this particular spot, the Holy Virgin appeared to them in a vision and told the abbot and his monks to return to the monastery, where a caravan of supplies would be waiting. They retraced their steps, and found that a hundred camels were assembled at the gateway, loaded with ample provisions. Questioned by the monks, the camel drivers explained that while camping at a place not far distant, they had found their camels miraculously loaded, and a beautiful lady ordered them to transport the supplies to the monastery.

Farther up, the route crosses a small ravine, and then passes through two rude gates. It is said that, formerly, monks were stationed at the first gateway to give passes to pilgrms who wished to go forward to take the sacrament on Mount Sinai. A steep climb up a somewhat crude flight of rocky steps made of huge slabs of granite leads on towards the summit. The steps were arranged with considerable skill by a monk called Moses, who reputedly built the whole stairway as a penance. Although the stones have been smoothed and leveled, mounting three thousand four hundred steps is, nevertheless, no mean feat. Another examination was made by a friar posted at the second gateway, at the very spot where, in remote days, Saint Stephen heard the confessions of pilgrims and gave them absolution before allowing them to proceed.

The second gateway opens onto a small plateau, the only stretch of level ground before the summit. Here, a huge cypress tree grows. It marks the spot where the Lord appeared to Elijah in fire and brimstone. Close by are two small buildings, both dedicated to Elijah. One is believed to have been built over the cave in which he sought refuge from the children of Israel who tried to kill him, and the other is beside a grotto in which he is believed to have concealed himself after he had slain the priests of the pagan god Baal. The chapel is used only once a year, when the monks make a solemn procession up the mountain to celebrate mass there.

From the chapel of Elijah, a continuation of the steps made by the monk called Moses leads up to the summit. On a platform of rock immediately below the summit is a natural hollow in the granite which bears a resemblance to the imprint of a camel's foot. It is regarded with great veneration by the Bedouin who call it *athar naget al Nabi*, or 'footprint of the Prophet's she-camel'. They associate it with the Prophet Muhammad's night journey to heaven.

A final climb of about a hundred steps leads to the summit of Mount Sinai. Here there are two granite buildings of modern date, a chapel and a mosque. The former is on the site of the original chapel erected by Justinian, which was destroyed and rebuilt many times. In the present chapel — which was designed with architectural details that are recognizably Justinianic incorporated into its structure — liturgy is performed by the monks on some Sundays. At the mosque, those of the Islamic faith sacrifice a sheep once a year, after celebrating the *mulid* of Nabi Saleh in the Wadi al Sheikh (p. 27).

The view from the summit is magnificent, especially at sunrise. Rugged, volcanic, precipitous gorges and gaunt pinnacles are lifted from darkness with the rising sun. Threadlike outlines turn into shapes. Subtle hues tint noble silhouettes, and peaks and ridges are touched with radiance. The air is rarefied, and the glowing sky casts light on what appears as a petrified ocean of lava. It is a noble panorama as viewed from this sacred place of long-standing tradition.

DESCRIPTION OF THE MONASTERY

Mount Catherine (Gebel Katrin)
The mountain that bears the name of the patron saint of the monastery in southern Sinai is so called because of the monastic legend that Saint Catherine's body was brought thither from Alexandria by angels. It is 2,642 meters high, and the highest peak in the whole peninsula. Because the summit peak is a huge naked block of granite descending steeply on all sides, it is easy to identify. The mountain lies south-west of Mount Sinai and can be approached from the Plain of Raha via Wadi al Laja. At the mouth of the valley leading to Mount Catherine are many early structures, including the Monastery of the Forty Martyrs (Deir al Arbain), which owes its name to the martyrs who were slain by the Blemmys (pp. 19, 36).

The base of Mount Catherine is extremely fruitful, with desert herbs and reeds providing nutritious feed for camels and goats. The foliage grows denser as one climbs upwards. A well, known as *Bir Shinnar* (Partridge Well), is a site with another tradition: monks making a pilgrimage to the summit were fainting from heat and thirst, when a partridge flew out of the well and guided them to this source of water.

The path up the mountain was also made by the monk Moses (p. 72), and is flanked by desert herbs and grasses growing in abundance, even on the upper slopes. It is a somewhat steep, but regular and picturesque climb until the ridge below the summit is reached. From this point on, the mountain is broken into a great many clefts and sturdy ledges that are, in fact, much simpler to negotiate than would appear from a distance. On the summit of Mount Catherine there is a small chapel built into the contours of the rockface and dedicated to the saint. It contains numerous icons, an apse adorned with representations of the Holy Virgin and Christ, and there is also a cavity in the bare rock at the southern end of the chapel which has been consecrated by the monks as the place where the saint's body was found. Adjoining the chapel are two rooms for pilgrims who wish to spend the night. The meteorological station was erected in 1932.

The view from the summit of Mount Catherine takes in a wider vista than that of Mount Sinai. In fact, on a clear day, almost three-quarters of the entire Sinai peninsula is visible, including the two gulfs, Suez and Aqaba, and the mountains of Africa to the west and Arabia to the east. Looking across the desert wastes, the monastery is out of sight, but what comes to mind are the Old Testament stories of biblical Sinai, the land of the exodus and the forty years of wandering in the wilderness.

Four
Biblical Sinai

The faith of the Christian Church is linked to the history of the countries of the eastern Mediterranean and western Asia. That is to say, the thoughts of the Hebrew prophets and judges, made known through their sacred Torah, were adopted by Christians as the Old Testament of their Holy Bible. Familiar to the Christian world today are those well-known Hebrew stories of our childhood: Joseph and the coat of many colors, Moses in the bulrushes, the exodus from Egypt, and the wanderings in Sinai.

Moses, to whom God revealed himself in the burning bush, and to whom the ten commandments were given, was born in Egypt of Canaanite parents and raised in the pharaoh's court. According to biblical accounts in Exodus, his first exposure to Sinai was when he fled there after incurring the wrath of the pharaoh by killing an Egyptian who caused suffering to the Hebrews. Moses probably escaped along the well-beaten track in northern Sinai, 'the Way of Shur', towards Midian, though exactly where this place was located is not known. After days of the fugitive life, Moses was resting by a well, when the daughters of Jethro, priest of Midian, came to water their father's flocks. Moses helped them, which courtesy they recounted to their father, who offered Moses hospitality and, subsequently, his daughter in marriage, and a new life in Midian. Moses accepted this new life, and settled into it happily — Zipporah bore him a son — until, "in process of time, ... the king of Egypt died". No doubt Moses heard of the death of the pharaoh, and considered returning to his own people in Egypt, but in any case the decision was taken out of his hands by the spectacular vision of the burning bush on Mount Horeb, which has been identified by biblical scholars with Mount Sinai. "And the angel of the Lord appeared unto him in a flame of fire out of the midst of a bush ... ", told him to remove his shoes because he was on holy ground — a detail which has captured the imaginations of believers, scholars and artists ever since — and commanded him to lead his people out of Egypt: "Come now therefore, and I will send thee unto Pharaoh, that thou mayest bring forth my people the children of Israel out of Egypt". His own inclinations thus given reassuring confirmation, Moses, with God guiding him, set out on his journey to Egypt, where he met his brother Aaron, whose eloquence persuaded the elders of the Hebrew community to adopt Moses' plan for their delivery out of Egypt, and "unto the land flowing with milk and honey".

A large community of foreigners from the Levant had long settled in the fertile triangle between the modern towns of Zagazig, Tell al Daba'a and Ismailia, an area that might have been the 'Land of Goshen' of biblical tradition. These settlers introduced different products into Egypt, including a new variety of sheep which produced better meat and wool than ever known before. Archaeological studies in recent years, have also uncovered sites of foreign settlement in areas other than the north-east delta region, discoveries which indicate the extent of the foreign culture in Egyptian territory. Among the immigrants were Hyksos, tribes from western Asia who controlled Egypt for a period of more than a hundred years from about 1786 B.C., and who set up their capital at Tell al Daba'a, and Canaanites who came as waves of immigrants, between 1720 and 1542 B.C., and especially after the expulsion of the Hyksos.

The Hyksos city of Avaris, or Pi-Ramses ('House of Ramses') was long identified with the ruins of the ancient city of Tanis in the north-eastern part of the Delta, where a large temple was discovered in the 1920s. It contained the ruins of a large number of statues, obelisks, sphinxes and stelae bearing the name of Ramses II and his successors, and the evidence seemed to confirm that Tanis was indeed the biblical bond-city. In the 1940s, however, a site was excavated some thirty kilometers south of Tanis, near the modern village of Khatana-Qantir. Tell al Daba'a proved to have the ruins of a royal palace and temples as well as pedestals to statues and obelisks, and Egyptologists are today able to confirm beyond doubt that Tell al Daba'a, and not Tanis, was the ancient Hyksos captial, and that Ramses II had simply transported the monuments there to give the impression, no doubt, that the city that bore his name was worthy of him! Be that as it may, Tell al Daba'a is the site that can be condfidently associated with biblical tradition; Tanis was, in fact, not built until later, in the eleventh century B.C.

Lacking historical evidence of the events that led to the exodus, one can only speculate on the possibility of the Egyptians levying heavy taxes on the settlers and forcing them to compulsory labor in, for example, the manufacture of bricks for the new delta capital, Pi-Ramses, the biblical Zoan. Without means to improve their lot, economically trapped in Egypt, treated as slaves, and resentful of their situation, the Hebrew people were only too happy to fall in with Moses' plan.

Most biblical historians agree that the exodus took place in the reign of Ramses II (1290-1224 B.C.) in the month of April. Apart from biblical sources, however, there is no evidence of this episode. The escape of a foreign tribe from Egypt was clearly far less important to the Egyptians than to the Hebrews who left. Ancient Egyptian texts, anyway, did not often concern themselves with minority groups.

It is difficult to estimate the number of people who left. According to Exodus it was three million. But archaeologist Flinders Petrie suggests that the number may have been much smaller because the word *alaf* means both a thousand, and a family; and by calculating an estimated number of fighting men and their dependants, Petrie concluded that the number of people may have been nearer twenty-seven thousand.

The route taken out of Egypt, and during the subsequent wanderings, has been a subject of debate since early

Christian times. Indeed, it is not even known exactly when Sinai became identified with the Sinai of the Bible. It would appear, however, that among the communities of hermits and monks who sought refuge in the peninsula from the third century, a tradition began to develop. It was not a firm tradition, because the holy people were not all in agreement, even among themselves, about the actual route, specific sites or, indeed, even on which of southern Sinai's many mountain peaks Moses actually received the law. The Bible itself refers to the 'mountain of God' as either Horeb or Sinai, nowhere making clear whether this was a single peak, two different mountains, or even the names used by different tribes to describe the same mountain.

In the nineteenth century, when Sinai became extremely popular amongst explorers in search of places related to the Bible, some effort was made to trace the exact sites of the wanderings. These researches were based, first, on documentary and inscriptional evidence and, second, on the geographical characteristics of the land. Among those who published opinions that were each, in turn, refuted, were J.L. Burckhardt, E. Robinson, H.S. Palmer, W.H. Bartlett, W.M.F. Petrie, Y. Aharoni, C.S. Jarvis, C. Beke, A. Musil, A. Lucas and D. Nielson. Even the exact point at which Moses crossed to Sinai could not be agreed upon. On this question there were three dominant views: the first was that they reached the Red Sea — which is supposed to have extended further north in biblical times — at or near Suez, and crossed to Ain Musa; the second, that they proceeded southwards on the Egyptian shore and crossed the waters of the Gulf of Suez at Ain Sukhna, moving across to Ain Musa; and the last, that they never came as far south as the Gulf of Suez at all, but traveled from the Nile delta towards Sinai along the Wadi Tumilat to Lake Timsah and the Bitter Lakes, where the crossing was made. This third opinion was the most generally accepted until the twentieth century.

Traditional Route of the Exodus
After crossing into Sinai, the Hebrews are believed to have come to what is still known as Ain Musa (the Spring of Moses). It is a small oasis that lies twenty-eight kilometers south of Suez, and tradition asserts that Moses and his people encamped there. In the writings of early travelers, the area is described as a beautiful oasis with fruit groves and a dozen or so perennial springs of brackish water rising through the soil. The site is today not so appealing.

Elim, the next stop, is described in Exodus as having twelve wells of water and seventy stems of palm trees. It has been identified with several sites including Wadi Garandel, Wadi Firan and al Tor. The first, Wadi Garandel, is a large and well-defined valley just north of the well-known sulfur springs at Hammam Faraon. There are numerous freshwater springs in the area that afford suitable watering places, and a succession of picturesque defiles through the valley, some with clusters of shady palms. Even today, after rainfall, depressions fill up with water, and little streams flow towards the valley, much as they undoubtedly did in ancient times.

The next encampment was the Wilderness of Sin, which has been identified with the large open plain of al Markha, where the Rudeis-Sidr oilfield is located now, ten kilometers south of Abu Zeneima. Here there is sparse vegetation, but at one corner of the plain, where the mountains break through the limestone cliffs, there is a sweetwater spring. Here, according to Exodus, the Hebrews were suffering from lack of food and drink and murmured against Moses in their weakness. Then the Lord said to Moses that He would "rain bread from heaven", and that the people could go out and gather it every day. And that evening quails flew over the camp, and in the morning dew lay on the ground. "And when the dew that lay was gone up, behold, upon the face of the wilderness there lay a small round thing ...," which the people did not know, but which Moses told them was "the bread which the Lord has given you to eat". Manna is a gummy substance tapped from the *tarfa* or tamarisk tree during just two months of the year (June and July) through the puncture hole of a small insect. The sap forms into white flax-like globules each day, is sweet to the taste, and can be gathered and kneaded into a palatable dough. The substance melts with the heat of the rising sun.

It is still a moot point whether Rephidem of the Bible, where the Hebrews went to next, is the Wadi Watia or, more probably, Wadi Firan, the picturesque and fertile area that was known to Victorian travelers as biblical Pharan, the Pearl of Sinai. Before the entrance to the oasis, a granite rock juts at an angle into the valley. Tradition holds that this was the very rock that yielded water when struck by Moses. Bounded, and so protected, by hills of red granite, the valley and the oasis are provided with abundant palms and scrub. The area is dominated by Mount Serbal, a 2,070-meter high mountain that stands alone on the plain. It is an imposing sight, and early Christian hermits at first thought that this mountain — which dwarfs all surrounding heights — was the Mount of the Law. Only later, when the monks of Firan Oasis joined

BIBLICAL SINAI

the community at Mount Sinai, did Mount Sinai become identified with the sacred site of the events described in the Bible. Nevertheless, because early Christian authorities like Eusebius and Cosmos had identified Serbal with Mount Horeb of the holy scriptures, it remained a site with a powerful tradition. Numerous caves in the area attest to the large numbers of hermits who lived in the oasis early in the Christian era.

Traveling eastwards from Wadi Firan, Moses led his people through a narrow defile, a long winding track through the pink granite and green diorite hills, where basalt and mica may have been scattered, as today, over the bed of the valley. From there they followed the course of what is now known as Wadi al Sheikh, until they advanced on the slightly inclined Plain of Raha, where they set up camp.

At an altitude of 800 meters, this plain is believed to be the place where Moses and his people encamped for an extended period of time. To the west of the plain is a hill, on a spur of which is a chapel believed to be the site where Aaron placed the golden calf, a graven image made of gold smelted from the jewelry collected from the Hebrew people, and before which offerings were made. Towards the north, the narrowing plain leads to Safsaf, hills with bold precipices which some biblical scholars thought was a more accessible point for Moses to have received the law.

From southern Sinai, Moses and his people made frequent journeys to Kadesh Barnea, a site in north-eastern Sinai that is strong in biblical tradition. Kadesh Barnea, present day Ain Gedeirat, is situated about six kilometers east of Kuseima, one of the oldest Bedouin settlements in the area known as Moses Valley. It is an extremely fertile area and it shares a tradition, with Wadi Firan, of being the site where Moses produced water from a rock. In fact, a strong stream flows through the valley and there is evidence of extensive cultivation and irrigation. A large stone reservoir, called *Bir Musa* (Moses' Well), provides no clues to its builders, but is generally regarded as of great antiquity. It is now dry, but catch basins can be seen as well as stone channels.

Northern Route of the Exodus
Despite fertile areas around valleys and oases in southern Sinai, vegetation is limited, and it is doubtful whether it could ever have been sufficient to sustain large numbers of people as well as vast herds of sheep and goats over a period of forty years. This observation by modern scholars, along with subsequent studies based on historic and geographical evidence, gave rise to the theory that Moses and the Hebrew tribes may have traveled, not to southern Sinai, but across northern Sinai by another route, or routes, to Kadesh Barnea where they remained for most of their wanderings.

To fit the theory, it was hypothesized that Moses led his people out of Egypt via Succoth (biblical Pithom, or present-day Tell al Maskuta), from which point they traveled along the Way of Shur across the dunes of northern Sinai to Mount Hilal, which was the Mount of the Law.

Another theory, based on recent archaeological studies in the north-eastern delta and on the northern coast of Sinai, has tended to support an even more northerly route. Moses led his people northward towards al Tina mud flats, to Lake Bardawil, which was the site of the crossing, and from there south to Kadesh Barnea of the Bible. Philologists have hastened to point out that *yam saf*, which has been translated into Red Sea, was actually the 'Sea of Reeds', the vast lakes on the Mediterranean coast between Port Said and al Arish. These are well over two meters below sea level and, moreover, have rushes and reeds on the southern shores that fit the biblical description. Furthermore, the northern coast is the only route for which a logical explanation can be presented for the drowning of the pharaoh's pursuing army; they could have been caught on the sandbars by the incoming tide.

Advocates of the northern routes have pointed out that ancient Egyptians occupied most of southern Sinai during the period of the Hebrew sojourn, because the turquoise and copper mines were located there, not only at Serabit al Khadim but at dozens of other sites. Indeed, there is evidence that southern Sinai was heavily garrisoned by Egyptian forces, and their barracks were within easy striking distance of the Plain of Raha and the Hebrew encampment.

Another observation that favors the northern route is that the tamarisk trees which produce the gum known as manna, are plentiful in northern Sinai, while they are few in the south. Finally, quails are common all along the Mediterranean coast, and they not infrequently land on the shore, or seek cover in the scrub during the autumn migration in September and October. In southern Sinai, however, quails are seldom seen, and certainly not in numbers sufficient to uphold the biblical description of feeding the multitude.

Perhaps the most convincing argument for the northern route for the exodus, is the fact that the only cultivable land large enough to support a horde of people, their goats and cattle, lies in the al Arish, Rafah, Kuseima triangle. This is in the same area as Kadesh Barnea of the Bible, where the twelve tribes are described as pitching their tents around the sacred tabernacle. Additionally, a number of names in northern Sinai strongly resemble places mentioned in Exodus, including Kadeis (Kadesh Barnea), Hazira (Hazeroth), Libni (Libnah) and Arish (Alush), whereas, in the south of the peninsula, the only arguable area may be Wadi Firan (the wilderness of Pharan).

As for a suitable Mount of the Law, northern Sinai is not lacking in this either. Mount Hilal is 892 meters high. The Arabic word *hilal* means 'crescent', but the word *halal* means 'lawful', in the context of ritual slaughter, or sacrifice, of animals. A confusion between these two words has maybe given rise to the suggestion that this mountain could have been the Mount of the Law of the Bible.

But historical facts and long-standing traditions frequently have a way of running at odds with one another. Evidence may result in the reevaluation of the former; but the endurance of the latter, even in the face of convincing argument, is remarkable. The conclusions of C.S. Jarvis in his *Yesterday and To-day in Sinai*, published sixty years ago, still apply today:

"On reading the wanderings, mention is found of the wilderness of Sinai, desert of Sinai, wilderness of Shur, wilderness of Paran, etc. These have been studied most carefully, and it is to be regretted that it is impossible to arrive at any conclusion as to where the Israelites imagined that these various wildernesses began and ended. The books of Exodus and Numbers are both vastly interesting, and marvellous examples of the literature of those days; but as a convincing road report they leave very much to be desired. It is absolutely impossible to map out correctly the route the Israelites took, and any attempt to do so leaves one completely fogged. The most one can do is more or less to trace these wanderings as far as the triangle El Arish-Rafa-Kosseima."

In fact, so long as people believe, and have faith, tradition will be perpetuated. Consequently, the sacred sites of southern Sinai, including the broad Plain of Raha and towering Mount Sinai, will continue to provide the focus of a tradition that will endure as long as pilgrims and visitors continue to make their way towards the Monastery of Saint Catherine on Mount Sinai.

Five
Getting There

Gone are the days when travelers to southern Sinai were well advised to take special care with their clothing and supplies, and to prepare themselves for a tiring journey across the desert. No longer are tedious formalities required to avail oneself of permits to satisfy customs and immigration authorities. Access to the Monastery of Saint Catherine is a simple matter of making the journey by air or road.

Air Sinai operates regular flights that take 45 minutes, with a shuttle service between the airport and the monastery. Zas Novotel near Cairo Airport also operates flights to southern Sinai. The coaches of the East Delta Bus Service operate daily from Abbasiya Terminal in Cairo. The journey is a long one, taking 6-8 hours, but the amenities of civilization are available at the end of the journey in the form of varied accommodation. The road, brilliantly engineered through the mountain areas, has a good surface, and petrol is available at all the big towns as well as near Saint Catherine's itself.

The main Suez highway from Heliopolis leads, 29 km. before Suez, to a turnoff (to the north) for the Ahmed Hamdi Tunnel which takes the road under the Suez Canal. The tunnel is some 7 km. north of the town of Suez, the distance from Heliopolis being about 120 km.

To the Monastery from the West
After crossing the Suez Canal into Sinai (toll of LE 1.00 through the Ahmed Hamdi Tunnel), a good quality road is signposted to al Tor, Sharm al Sheikh and Saint Catherine's. (From the tunnel there are two parallel roads, about 1 km. apart, which lead south and join after about 12 km. There is little advantage of one route over the other.) The road then follows the west coast of the Sinai Peninsula for 115 km. before swinging inland (a short spur continuing to Hammam Faraon) rejoining the coast 35 km. later at Abu Zeneima, then continuing to the south of Abu Rudeis where, 194 km. from the tunnel, the road again turns sharply inland. After a further 12 km. another turn sharp left leads away from the al Tor road toward Saint Catherine's, Nuweiba, and Taba along the lower part of the Wadi Firan.

The drive inland, from the turn off the al Tor road up to Saint Catherine's Monastery, is a most impressive scenic drive. After passing through Firan Oasis, some 45 km. from the coast, with its habitation, gardens and traces of early

GETTING THERE

Christian buildings, the road begins to climb, and there is a fine prospect of Mount Serbal, its many peaks clear against the sky and dwarfing all surrounding heights. The road continues to climb through the Wadi al Sheikh to the Watia Pass (292 km. from the tunnel), a narrow defile some 18 km. north of the monastery. Here the mountains are of many hues, ranging from chocolate brown and violet to yellow and white, and acacia bushes border the cliffs. A gas station 7 km. farther on marks the turn-off for the airport (and Nuweiba). Ahead the road continues for the last 10 km. through a narrowing valley between the towering mountains. Landmarks are the tomb of Nabi Saleh, the Zeituna campground and finally the crossroads at the center of the Saint Catherine's locale. Ahead lies the local village of Saint Catherine's. The monastery is situated in its valley 3 km. to the south-east, and the Saint Catherine's Tourist Village immediately to the north-west.

The distance from the tunnel to the al Tor/Wadi Firan junction is 206 km., and from there to Saint Catherine's is a further 103 km. The journey can be completed quite comfortably by private car in just over 3 hours (440 km., and less than 5 hours from central Cairo).

To the Monastery from the East
For travelers with a less hurried itinerary, and especially for those who have been to Sharm al Sheikh or Nuweiba, Saint Catherine's can also be approached from the east. Some 33 km. south of Nuweiba, and 37 km. north of Dahab, lies the junction of the road across southern Sinai. Turn to the west to reach the monastery.

For the next 85 km. the mountain scenery is in a class of its own, even more impressive than the approach from

GETTING THERE

the west. The road winds its way through incredible landscapes. Wadi Watia, which travels a winding course of some 18 km., is of varying widths, and appears, in parts, to be chiseled out of the eroding mountains. The crumbling walls of the valley rise vertically from rock-strewn bed to purple peak, totally blocking out the sun in places. There appears to be little life, just the remnants of age-old landslides of stone, and a few spiny bushes. This is one of the wildest and most dramatic of the dry river beds of southern Sinai, with evidence of flash floods up to 3 m. high in rock pools that once trapped the water.

Forward planning will be well rewarded if this journey is timed for the early part of the day, to avoid having the sun in one's eyes.

Where to Stay
Apart from the accommodation at the Monastery of Saint Catherine already described on p. 61, there are tourist facilities and campsites. For modern comfort, the Tourist Village of Saint Catherine is an attractive resort, built of natural stone and designed to blend aesthetically with the surrounding landscape. It has comfortable air-conditioned chalet suites with all modern facilities, and a good restaurant. There is a new Coffee Shop, 'al Monaga', by the crossroads on the edge of the village, which offers a full range of meals and refreshments.

For the hardier visitor, there are several campsites, including Zeituna Camp which lies 6 km. north of the monastery, and has cots and blankets in stone-walled 'tents'. The so-called 'Fairuz Hotel', recently opened beyond the Tourist Village, appears to offer only rudimentary facilities.

GETTING THERE

Distances

Saint Catherine - Cairo	440 km.
Saint Catherine - Canal tunnel	309 km.
Saint Catherine - al Tor	163 km.
Saint Catherine - Sharm al Sheikh	265 km.
Saint Catherine - Dahab	127 km.
Saint Catherine - Nuweiba	106 km.
Saint Catherine - Taba	188 km.

Selected Bibliography

Bassili, W.F. *Sinai and the Monastery of Saint Catherine.* Cairo, 1961.

Bentley, James. *Secrets of Mount Sinai: The Story of the World's Oldest Bible - Codex Sinaiticus.* Doubleday Inc. New York, 1986.

Dobson, A. *Mount Sinai. A Modern Pilgrimage.* London, 1925.

Dumas, J. *La Péninsule du Sinai.* Cairo, 1951.

Eckenstein, L. *A History of Sinai.* London, 1921.

Evans, C.F. *Resurrection and the New Testament.* London, 1970.

Farmer, W.F. *The Last Twelve Verses of Mark.* Cambridge, 1974.

SELECTED BIBLIOGRAPHY

Forsyth, C. and Weitzmann, K. *The Monastery of Saint Catherine: The Church and Fortress of Justinian.* Princeton, 1973.

Gerster, Georg. *Sinai: Terre de la Revelation.* Frankfurt A.M., 1961.

Jarvis, C.S. *Yesterday and To-day in Sinai.* London, 1931.

Jones, A.H.M. *The Later Roman Empire, 284-602. A Social, Economic and Administrative Survey.* University of Oklahoma Press, 1964.

Meinardus, O. *Christian Egypt Ancient and Modern.* The American University in Cairo Press, 1977.

Palmer, E.H. *The Desert of the Exodus.* Cambridge, 1871.

Prescott, H.F.M. *Once to Sinai.* London, 1957.

Rabino, H.L. *Le Monastère de Sainte-Catherine du Mont Sinaï.* Cairo, 1938.

Rothenberg, B. and Weyer, H. *Sinai.* Trans. by E. Osers and B. Charleston. Washington and New York, 1980.

Tischendorf, K. von. *Die Sinai Bibel.* Liepzig, 1871.

Weitzmann, K. *The Monastery of Saint Catherine at Mount Sinai: The Icons, from the sixth to the tenth century.* Princeton University Press, 1976.

Index

Aaron 83
Abu Zeneima 13
accommodation 61-62, 91
Ain Gedeirat 83
Ain Musa 7, 32, 81
Ain Sukhna 7
Alexander II (czar of Russia) 49, 64, 66, 67
Alexander the Great 6
Alexandria 74
  Catechetical School 2
  Church of Saint Catherine 23
Alush 86
Amr ibn al As 6

Antiochus 6
Aqaba 10
al Arish 9, 86
Assyrians 6
Avaris 78

Baldwin I (king of Jerusalem) 28
Bedouin 10, 14-15, 19, 27, 31, 37, 70, 73
bell tower 42, 52
Blemmys 19, 36, 74
British 6, 14, 33
burning bush 12, 19, 44, 46, 76, 77

95

INDEX

Cambyses 6
Canaanites 78
Catechetical School (Alexandria) 2
Catherine the Great 35
cemetery 61
chapels 19, 32, 42, 46, 50, 72, 74
  Burning Bush 49-50
  Saint George 69
  Saint Tryphon 60-61
  Virgin Mary 71
Charles VI (king of France) 35
charnel house 60-61
Church of Saint Catherine (Alexandria) 23
Church of Saint George (al Tor) 36
Church of the Transfiguration 21, 24, 30, 44-49
Clement 2
Codex Alexandrinus 63, 66
Codex Ephraem 63
Codex Sinaiticus 34, 54, 63-69
Codex Syriacus 53
Codex Vaticanus 63, 66, 68
Constantine (king of Greece) 36
Constantine (Roman emperor) 18, 68
Constantinople 1, 20, 56, 57, 68
Council of Constantinople 27
Council of Chalcedon 2, 20
Council of Nicea 26

Covenant of the Prophet 25
Crete 58
Crusaders 6, 24, 28, 45, 57

Darb al Hajj 10

Egyptian Wildlife Service 16
Elim 81
emperors
  Constantine 18, 68
  Decius 22
  Diocletian 22
  Justinian 20, 37, 41, 73
  Leo III 26
  Maximanus 22
  Theodosius III 54
Epiphanius 26
Etheria 19
Eusebius 68, 83
Eutychios 18
exodus 6, 75, 76, 79-86
  northern routes 84-86
  traditional route 81-84

feasts 62
Firan Oasis 6, 12, 20, 25, 26, 29, 82, 89. *See also* Wadi Firan.
flight into Egypt 6
Forty Martyrs 20, 36, 74
French 6, 32

garden 60
Gaza 9
Gebel Katrin *see* Mount Catherine
Gebel Musa *see* Mount Sinai

96

INDEX

Gebeliya 37, 52
Goshen 78
guest quarters 42, 61
Gulf of Aqaba 7
Gulf of Suez 7, 13

al Hakim (Fatimid caliph) 51
Hammam Faraon 81
Hazeroth 86
Hazira 86
Helena 18, 21
hermits 12, 19, 20, 25, 31, 70
Hyksos 78

icon collection 55-59
iconoclasm 26, 55
icons 42, 44, 46, 47, 52, 75
income and holdings 35-36
Isabella (queen of Spain) 35
Islam 5, 10, 25, 28, 37, 71

Jerusalem 28
Jethro 44, 77
Judaism 70
Justinian (Roman emperor) 20, 37, 41, 73

Kadeis 86
Kadesh Barnea 83, 84, 85, 86
Khatana-Qantir 78
Kléber Tower 33, 41
Kuseima 83

Lake Bardawil 8, 16, 84
Libnah 86
Libni 86
library 42, 53

Louis IX (king of France) 24
Louis XI (king of France) 35
Louis XIV (king of France) 35

Maghara 13
Mamluks 10, 32
manuscripts 53-54, 69
al Markha 81
Maximilian (emperor of Germany) 35
Midian 77
mosaic 48-49
Moses 6, 19, 44, 50, 71, 76-85
Moses' Well 44, 84
mosque (in the Monastery) 27, 42, 50-52
Mount Catherine 7, 23, 27, 40, 74-75
Mount Hilal 84, 86
Mount Horeb 71, 77, 80, 83
Mount of the Law 6, 12, 82, 84, 86
Mount Serbal 82, 90
Mount Shayib 7
Mount Sinai 16, 23, 33, 41, 70-73, 80
Muhammad 25, 27, 51
Muhammad Ali 35

Nabi Saleh 27, 73, 90
Nakhl 10
Napoleon 6, 32-33

Origen 2
ossuary 60-61

97

INDEX

Pachomius, Father 42
Pantaenus 2
Pelusium 8
persecutions 12, 22
Persians 6
Peter the Great (czar of Russia) 49
Pharan 12, 20, 82, 86
Pharaoh 77
pharaohs 5, 9
  Ramses II 5, 78, 79
  Thutmose III 5
Phoenicians 9
Pi-Ramses 78, 79
pilgrims
  Christian 6, 12, 18-21, 33, 52, 57, 75
  Muslim 10, 33
Pithom 84
Plain of Raha 71, 83, 85
plateau of al Tih 9, 10
popes
  Honorius III 29
  Innocent IV 29

Rafah 8, 9
Ras Muhammad 13, 16
refectory 52
relics
  burning bush 50
  Saint Basil 46
  Saint Catherine 24, 29, 30, 49
  Saint Gregory of Nyssa 46
  Saint John Chrysostom 46
Rephidem 82
Roberts, David 34

Safaga 13
saints
  Basil 1
  Catherine 21-24, 37, 74
  George 37
  Gregory I the Great 21
  Gregory of Tours 21
  Holy Virgin 71-72
  John Klimakos 45, 54
  Pachomius 1
  Stephanos 61, 72
Serabit al Khadim 13, 85
Sharm al Sheikh 13
Simeon I (archbishop of Sinai) 28
Sinai in biblical tradition 3, 6, 12, 30, 44, 75, 76-87
Succoth 84
Suez Canal 14, 15
Sultan Selim 31

Taba 13
tablets of the law 71
Tanis 78
Tell al Daba'a 78
Tell al Maskuta 84
ten commandments 71, 76
al Tina 84
al Tor 19, 27, 29, 36, 81
Turks 6, 31, 32, 33

Verame, Jean 38
von Tischendorf, Konstantin 34, 64-69

Wadi al Deir 71
Wadi al Laja 71

INDEX

Wadi al Sheikh 73, 83, 90
Wadi Arish 10
Wadi Bir Nafekh 38
Wadi Firan 19, 27, 32, 36, 81, 82, 83, 84, 86.
  See also Firan Oasis.
Wadi Garandel 32, 81
Wadi Watia 82, 91
Wallachians 21, 37

wars 14-15
Watia Pass 90
Way of Horus 8
Way of Shur 77, 84
Wilderness of Sin 81

Zipporah 44, 77
Zoan 79

INDEX

Wadi al Sheikh 73, 85, 90
Wadi Arabah 10
Wadi el-Tufah, 58
Wadi Feiran 19, 27, 32, 39, 81,
82, 85, 84, 86
See also Firan Oasis
Wadi Gharndel 52, 81
Wadi Watia 82, 91
Wallachians 27, 77

wars 14-15,
Watia Pass 90
Way of Horus 6
Way of Shur 77, 81
Wilderness of Sin 81

Zipporah 45, 77
Zoar 77